Critique of Digitality

Jan Distelmeyer

Critique of Digitality

palgrave
macmillan

Jan Distelmeyer
Europäische Medienwissenschaft
Potsdam University of Applied Sciences/University of Potsdam
Potsdam, Brandenburg, Germany

ISBN 978-3-658-36977-4   ISBN 978-3-658-36978-1 (eBook)
https://doi.org/10.1007/978-3-658-36978-1

© Springer Fachmedien Wiesbaden GmbH, part of Springer Nature 2022
This book is a translation of the original German 1st edition Kritik der Digitalität by Jan Distelmeyer, published by Springer Fachmedien Wiesbaden GmbH, part of Springer Nature in 2021. The translation was done with the help of artificial intelligence (machine translation by the service DeepL.com). The author (with the friendly support of Simon Vincent) has subsequently revised the text further in an endeavour to refine the work stylistically.
This work is subject to copyright. All rights are reserved by the Publisher, whether the whole or part of the material is concerned, specifically the rights of translation, reprinting, reuse of illustrations, recitation, broadcasting, reproduction on microfilms or in any other physical way, and transmission or information storage and retrieval, electronic adaptation, computer software, or by similar or dissimilar methodology now known or hereafter developed.
The use of general descriptive names, registered names, trademarks, service marks, etc. in this publication does not imply, even in the absence of a specific statement, that such names are exempt from the relevant protective laws and regulations and therefore free for general use.
The publisher, the authors, and the editors are safe to assume that the advice and information in this book are believed to be true and accurate at the date of publication. Neither the publisher nor the authors or the editors give a warranty, expressed or implied, with respect to the material contained herein or for any errors or omissions that may have been made. The publisher remains neutral with regard to jurisdictional claims in published maps and institutional affiliations.

This Palgrave Macmillan imprint is published by the registered company Springer Fachmedien Wiesbaden GmbH, part of Springer Nature.
The registered company address is: Abraham-Lincoln-Str. 46, 65189 Wiesbaden, Germany

Acknowledgements

This little book has quite a long history. Its publication—initially in German—is first and foremost due to the initiative and openness of Ivo Ritzer, without whom the attempt to tackle such an expansive topic in a rather narrow framework would not have happened. The English translation was made possible by the support and wise advice of Simon Vincent, who has thought through linguistic and content issues together in an illuminating way for this practice of theory. The group of friends and colleagues whose suggestions have been incorporated in this book is so large that it is impossible for me to thank them individually in this context. Nevertheless, I would like to express my special gratitude for the regular exchange with students and teachers in Potsdam, in the research college "Sensing—The Knowledge of Sensitive Media" and in the research group "Interfaces" of the German Society for Media Studies. In particular, I would like to thank Till A. Heilmann, Timo Kaerlein and Florian Sprenger for their reading and criticism of the individual chapters. More than thanks I owe to Bettina and Pina Distelmeyer for their support, for our conversations and everything.

Contents

1 **Digitality and Critique** 1
   1.1 Digitality (Programmatic Interactions) 1
   1.2 Myth/Matter (Digitalicity and Computerisation).. 11
   1.3 Discourse (Indefinite Definition) 18
   1.4 Friendly Takeover (the Net) 27
   1.5 Critique 33
   1.6 ... of Digitality (Unfolding Concerns) 43

2 **Interface and *Leiten*** 51
   2.1 Interfaces (Levels of Connections) 51
   2.2 *Leiten* (Make Go) 58
   2.3 Power (Commanding and Complying) 62
   2.4 Depresenting (Conceal and Disclose) 70
   2.5 Interfacing (Conducting and Guiding) 76
   2.6 Question Mode (Interface Analyses) 82

3 **Programme and Everyday Life** 93
   3.1 Participation (Intermediate Spaces) 93
   3.2 App Order (Objects and Processes) 101
   3.3 Always on (Era of Software Power) 109
   3.4 No Conclusion (Mistrust and Decision-Making).. 117

References 121

Digitality and Critique 1

1.1 Digitality (Programmatic Interactions)

Digitality is an imposition. This does not contradict the advantages of digital technology. Nor does it contradict the facilitation, assistance and productivity from which people profit in ever-increasing areas of their lives through the use of computers and their connectivity. Rather, the imposition and challenge follow precisely in tandem with the growing spread and importance of this form of technology and the easing of workloads associated with it along with its processes of automation, which furthermore, and in a quite particular way, liberates us from having to understand the processes involved.

The concept of digitality focuses on something fundamental. It marks, first of all, a humanities-based perspective on the totality of the far-reaching and deep-rooted developments that may also be summarised as computerisation. Therein lies the commonality of the various notions of digitality: Namely, the totality and peculiarity of the conditions and consequences of electronic digital computing in all its forms. Thus, digitality becomes an imposition and challenge for at least four reasons, which—since they are both constraining *and* illuminating—I would like to explore and discuss before anything else.

These four elements of imposition both determine and structure the first four steps of this chapter. The ambition of the term digitality, along with the simultaneous presence and concealment of (pre)conditions, apparatuses and processes all signify the first imposition (i.e. *programmatic interactions*). From the interaction of mythical and material factors follows the second imposition (i.e. *myth/matter*), which is followed by the third (*discourse*) that consists of the different theoretical approaches to digitality. Finally, the fourth imposition (*the network*), which is also discursive, concerns the recent tendency to equate "digital" automatically together with "networked".

Out of these four steps, I will go on to develop, in this first chapter, a concept of critique. It is conceived here as an unfolding of concerns, for which I will use the interface concept and the German term "leiten" in the following chapters. While the interface concept addresses various forms of relations thanks to which computers function, are networked and establish relations with the world beyond the computer, *leiten* refers in an equal and thus untranslatable manner to processes of physical conducting as well as idea-related leading and guiding. This is why the interaction of both terms seems to me to be extremely helpful in responding to the challenge of digitality. The brief introduction to a critique of digitality that this volume offers is thus an introduction both to an engagement with the (pre)conditions and consequences of electronic digital computing and to the challenges of such an endeavour. Therefore, I would like to start with the question of what the concept of digitality actually entails and helps to address.

The claim of digitality to grasp a totality of fundamentals and effects conceptually poses the first challenge, a Sisyphean task of tracing both the versatility and development of a technology whose celebrated strength lies precisely in its permanent changeability. Computer technology can and will, as its programmability guarantees, adapt itself to the most diverse ends. Continuous changes: Tracing and attempting to understand the conditions, apparatuses, processes, and consequences associated with buzzwords such as "digital revolution," "digitalisation," and epochs such as the "digital age" is, therefore, an ongoing occupation, with only those who wish to ignore the increasing influence of this technology doubting that such a task is necessary. If digitality is indeed commonplace, so its critique, its analysis and assessment, should also be.

1.1 Digitality (Programmatic Interactions)

Just how much this task requires can be demonstrated by the fact that, on the one hand, digital technology (and its logic) provides a kind of central focus or cohesion, while on the other, however, any idea of a conceptual unity is certainly misleading. For what we find under the glossy and catch-all term of "digitalisation" is highly diverse. Different processes, leading principally to concentrated and networked automation and acceleration, are rapidly becoming operative in several different realms, shaping educational institutions as well as industries, ecology as well as the economy, social behaviour as well as warfare and many other parts of not only human life.

Furthermore the tendency to bring together the most diverse processes, "which were previously addressed under the umbrella of terms such as 'social change' or 'technical progress' currently, under the hardly less-incoherent, highly de-differentiating collective term 'digital transformation'"(Krajewski 2019, p. N4), is a tendency that continues to grow. Indeed it reached a new peak in the spring of 2020 during the COVID-19 pandemic, especially among those voices that have since filed away misgivings as mere "debates about taste" as a result of it becoming clearly manifest how digitalisation is a "gift for humanity" (von Gehlen 2020) and how it had become "our refuge" (Rosenfeld 2020): "The digital now binds us together." (ibid.)

I will return to effect of the coronavirus in the course of the first chapter when considering all four elements of imposition. For the handling of the pandemic has vividly reinforced the blurring and overlapping of these terms, as I intend to outline in the first four steps of this chapter.

Initially, however—thus looping back to the first imposition of simultaneous presence and concealment—the desired ubiquity of computer technology is almost impossible to keep track of, and not just because of its vast proliferation. It is overwhelming and not only on account of its networked dispersion and embedding of itself into so many realms of far more than human life, encompassing, for example, computerised smart cities as well as a "hiveopolis" (APA 2019), hives with computerised sensory technologies. Moreover, this connected proliferation is occurring in tandem with a diversification of digital apparatuses, the sheer scope of whose forms is also expanding very rapidly.

The path leading from room-sized mainframe computers to home and personal computers, and from laptops to tablet computers, smart phones, smart wristwatches or even smart glasses is but one part of this complex aimed decidedly at humans. At the same time, the literal embedding of computer technologies continues in objects found in the Internet of Things, in machines and in bodies (for example in the form of pacemakers, hearing aids or RFID chips embedded under the skin of animals and humans). Their automation is designed to include a certain momentum that potentially takes humans out of the equation. In the case of autonomous and connected vehicles as well as "autonomous weapons" (Scharre 2018), this is still a highly controversial topic, although the "algorithmic trading" (Reichert 2009, pp. 69–74) of automated high-frequency stock exchanges has been part of everyday life for years.

In addition to the extensive proliferation and diversification of computer technologies, there is a fundamental property of computers that puts yet another strain on the task of creating an overview, one that makes it a somewhat ungraspable concept. How do we survey machines whose ambition is "universality"? How can an overview comprehend a General Purpose Machine, that "really all-purpose automatic digital computing system" (von Neumann 1993, p. 39), whose lack of purpose is paradoxically focussed on a single purpose, namely to compute? Furthermore, how can this overview succeed if such ongoing computing processes ultimately consist of "manipulating series upon series of characters according to unambiguous rules" (Coy 1994, p. 19), thanks to processors running at inhuman speeds that keep switching circuits through electrical impulses acting on the commands of a given programme? In other words: How can I recognise the very thing that in this way (increasingly) eludes observability?

This challenge that digitality imposes is related to a fundamental and, by way of intermediation, bridged difference: When dealing with computers, the observable and the unobservable are *programmatically* interconnected—and *programmatic* refers to both the concrete realisation of programmes and the underlying programmability that so fundamentally distinguishes computers from other technologies. Unobservable processes in and between

1.1 Digitality (Programmatic Interactions)

computers are reciprocally connected with manifestations and perceptible effects of these internal programme and processor performances. Since the beginnings of electronic digital computers with instruction memories in the late 1940s, it has been necessary to mediate between the computational processes in the machine and what, as input or output, either instructs these processes or results from them.

This fundamental condition of processes has been discussed repeatedly as a kind of contradictory, oppositional coupling. In the mid-1980s, Frieder Nake (2021/1984, pp. 279–287) characterised the computer principle as one of doubling: The function of computers accessible to us is to operate both mediated and unmediated, and inaccessible facilitating the "machinisation of work performed by the human brain." In the late 2010s, Sybille Krämer (2018, p. 41) described the "Janus face" of "networked digitality" thus: In front of the user interfaces, "users can generate knowledge from the net in a more self-empowering way than ever before" by writing/reading. Behind all of this, however, lies "a realm of algorithms, protocols and devices communicating with each other so vast that it is barely controllable any more by user power".

The spheres of influence of such a coupling are in turn expanding and intensifying their own interactions, which, on the one hand, are characterised by the existence of and interaction with apparatuses and infrastructures, as can be visibly evidenced by the proliferation of mobile computers as smartphones. On the other hand, however, this present era of digitality is at the same time characterised by the power of hidden processes of *leiten*, calculating, instructing and controlling particularly emphasised in the developments and discussions around artificial intelligence and machine learning, on smart cities and Big Data.

The buzzword Big Data "first appeared in an academic publication in 2003", aiming at the big (and hoped-for) picture, yet it "only gained broader legitimacy around 2008" (Boellstorff 2014, p. 107), as it concerns the largest possible quantities of data. Such a mass of data, collected for example by registering activities on the internet or in cities, exceeds human comprehension. Thus, software applications that make as the basis of their operations the recording of as many connections and relations as possible are highly attractive. *Too big to fail*: The automatic evaluations of these vast data volumes and the results of data mining, promise both diagnostic precision and predictive miracles.

Concepts behind smart cities build on this, but not as a new phenomenon since "networked or computable cities began to appear as regular features in urban development plans from the 1980s onwards" (Gabrys 2014, p. 32). Such cities and other systems become "intelligent" insofar as their activities can be automatically recorded and, in the case of traffic flow, for example, regulated and directed thanks to sensor-enhanced computer technology. Intelligence is thus taken to mean here the ability to automatically and programmatically process the data that remains of the world once all necessary processes of formalisation have taken place.

The computer application of machine learning, understood as AI (artificial intelligence) and which was pushed forward in the 2010s, further expands on the concept of Big Data as both an exemplary and probability-calculating extrapolation of the past. The goal of these learning techniques is "to enable a computer to learn from experience in order to solve specific tasks and make predictions without having been explicitly programmed to perform this function" (Sudmann 2018a, p. 10). Patterns are detected within past situations and events, from which probabilistic assessments and decisions are derived in order to negotiate future ones. The special feature of this prediction technology, however, is that these machine learning programmes are considered successful and productive if they are proven to be correct in the tests on data already collected, so that their first task is not at all to predict the future, but the past (cf. Chun 2021). Determined to self-determine. What is referred to here as learning and intelligence is a specialised, automated quasi-independence which must first be created, aligned and trained by a third party. It requires exact preparation and maintenance. Therefore—because properties such as autonomy and self-reliance assume a freedom of will, which computers do not possess—this quasi-self-reliance could be more accurately called a programmatic autonomy, a new dynamic based on programmability. This quasi-autonomy involves automatic, not

1.1 Digitality (Programmatic Interactions)

explicitly prescribed processes, for which it nevertheless needs its own programmatic and conditional frameworks.

For the same reason, there is much to be said for using the term "artificial intelligence" with caution. Since the term intelligence "invokes connotations of a human-like autonomy and intentionality that should not be ascribed to machine-based procedures", the AlgorithmWatch initiative has suggested speaking here instead of processes of *algorithmic decision-making,* of "algorithmically controlled, automated decision-making (ADM)" (Alfter/Müller-Eiselt/Spielkamp 2019, p. 9).

AI's learning processes, or more precisely ADM systems, are trained by human input, where artificial neural networks are fed with data. One highly important function is performed by the micro-tasks of crowdworking and clickworking, in which large numbers of people label images or read out texts, for example, in order that an information-processing system can detect and develop a library of speech patterns and image recognition which it will deploy in future scenarios; this form of AI will, in turn, be further optimised by human, everyday computer use. Of great interest here is that it goes unnoticed, for example, that the pre-trained models for image recognition run in the background on my smartphone, while "at night, during charging phases, the images taken during the day are analysed and processed using, among other things, facial recognition models" (Engemann 2018, p. 253).

Thus, the everyday relationship between humans and computers is by no means limited to what people do with computers through their conscious and intentional actions. Rather, it is characterised by complex ostensible and hidden interactions. Even in the now commonplace example of "digital photography," those "little computers" that are digital cameras engage in more than one relationship with the information they capture in that they "record, process, transmit, distribute, display, and store" (Gerling/Holschbach/Löffler 2018, p. 81). Such interactions are shaping more and more forms of computers that are designed to capture life, measure it, and make it the very object of data production and distribution.

Hayles (2016, p. 33) has called this development of programmatic autonomy and agency "the third wave of computation", after the mainframe supercomputers located in workplaces in the mid-twentieth century, and the worldwide adoption of personal computers (PCs) in the 1980s. This third wave is rooted in particular in the proliferation and embedding of a great variety of sensors, which record whatever it is that can be recorded using these technologies and turn it into processable data. Around twenty sensors in a current smartphone (from the microphone and GPS to the accelerometer) ensure that such networked computers constitute the most commonplace examples of such sensory and not always conscious relationships between humans and computers. Together they belong to the practices of sensing (cf. Angerer et al. 2018; Gabrys 2019), referring to an interweaving of human and computer modes of detecting and evaluating.

The fact that my smartphone permanently and precisely records then relays my movements is perhaps only apparent and useful to me personally when I can use it to locate both my position and direction of movement when using a navigation app. Quite who else benefits from this—the police, PR companies or those detecting the early onset of Parkinson's, since movements can be tracked in depth, subtlety and detail (cf. Arora et al. 2014)—is a question of not only interest and concern, but also access and accountability. "When I'm talking to my wife," computer scientist Iyad Rahawan (2019, p. 102) states, describing his discomfort with everyday sensing processes, "sometimes an advertisement appears on my laptop shortly afterward that matches the content of our conversation."

During the COVID-19 pandemic, sensing processes were used worldwide and aggressively from March 2020 onwards. Various nations secured access to the smartphone data of their inhabitants and reacted to the coronavirus with "mass surveillance" (Föderl-Schmid and Hurz 2020). In Germany, the Robert Koch Institute, as an independent higher federal authority, asked users of fitness bracelets and smartwatches in early April 2020 to use voluntarily the "Corona Data Donation App" (cf. Fig. 2.5). Vital data on, for example, a user's resting pulse and activities, which these "wearables" record thanks to their in-built sensors, are intended to help

1.1 Digitality (Programmatic Interactions)

"better record and understand the spread of the coronavirus" (RKI 2020a). Provided with gender, age, weight, height and postcode information, the app automatically makes the data collected on "sleep patterns, heart rates and body temperatures" available to the Robert Koch Institute "voluntarily and pseudonymously" (ibid.). Criticisms of this procedure, in which pseudonymisation only takes place "after the RKI has already received the data in full" (Biselli and Tschirsich 2020), were centred around issues of data protection and feared for the "total and location-specific monitoring of users' bodily functions" (Bock et al. 2020, 34). Similar problems—above all the question of whether collected data should be stored and managed centrally or de-centrally (cf. D64 et al. 2020; BMG 2020)—shaped the debate surrounding the "Corona Tracing App" developed on behalf of the German government: This software, uses a smartphone's Bluetooth interface not to capture location data or movement profiles (tracking), but to reconstruct possible contact with infected persons (tracing). Smartphones are thus developing into a key technology for existential questions concerning health, government and democracy.

Thanks to such sensor-enhanced machines, not only what humans can perceive and know about computers is changing, but also what computers perceive and know about people, or more precisely: What they can capture, measure and transfer. Sensors, as elements and interfaces of computers, extend their reach and effect far beyond the boundaries of established user interfaces. They capture and process (their) environments and are thus involved not only in the production of data, but also of new relationships (cf. Gabrys 2016).

Hidden—that is, withdrawn from both view and access—are thus a number of components that make the contemporary complex of digitality indeed functional and effective, however at the same time difficult to grasp or manage. Hidden are the underground and underwater cables of the internet, hidden are the sealed-off server parks, hidden are the inner workings of my computer, that material organisation of circuit boards, slots, chips, cards, processor units, and wires that I don't get to see, in part, as unauthorised opening of the equipment violates my obligations under the machine's warranty agreement.

Hidden differently are the programming's procedures and presuppositions. The algorithms behind recommendation automation on platforms such as Netflix, Spotify and Amazon, or for the newsfeed on Facebook, are just as much a part of this as the choice already made available when the user launches them, along with samples of user preferences with which artificial neural networks are trained (cf. Caliskan et al. 2017). The same is true for the premises of Big Data analytics. Their guiding idea has been described by Wendy Chun (2018, pp. 131–132) as "homophily", on the basis of which analytics can "divide users into segregated neighborhoods based on *likes* and *dislikes*."

Finally—not forgetting the switching circuits already mentioned—all those forms of actual signal transfer and its processing within and between computers remain hidden. Their working processes not only elude our human observation but increasingly also our comprehension. The metaphor of the *black box,* "an opaque technical apparatus for which only the inputs and outputs are known" (Galloway 2011, p. 239) sounds very familiar in this context. Mind the gap: Machine learning methods are repeatedly described in current debates "as opaque black-box technology, i.e. as technical systems that can only be accessed via their respective inputs and outputs, since their internal operations are at least partly opaque, i.e. beyond human comprehension." (Sudmann 2018b, p. 63).

As obvious and obscure, as far-reaching and profound as this proliferation and diversification of computer technology is, so great is the challenge facing the concept of digitality to address the totality and peculiarity of this complex. This is not something that can be escaped simply by strategically limiting proposed ambitions, for example, to those manifestations of computer technology that are current and visible to people and subsequently confer on them the status of "user". For the scope and dimensions of this part of digitality are already vast. Consider, for example, the operations of an "Industry 4.0" (BMWi 2014), the social and political effects of social media and the internet as the basis of new economic orders, as discussed under terms such as "Wikinomics" (Tapscott 2007), "Communicative Capitalism" (Dean 2008), "Sharing Economy" (Taeihagh 2017) and many others.

However, the fact that this strategic restriction is not a restriction at all, but rather a mere detour leading to the same complexity, is due to the fundamental interconnection of explicit user interaction and implicit processes. These programmatic interactions become intensified the more the operations of computers are facilitated and shaped by their own interconnectivity. The presence of smartphones testifies to the simultaneity of both these phenomena, in that the very functionality of the devices at hand is contingent on concealed network processes.

1.2 Myth/Matter (Digitalicity and Computerisation)

The ambitious claim of the term to be able to get a categorical grip on such a (over-)demanding complexity marks the first imposition and challenge of digitality. The second challenge that faces us concerning digitality is differently linked to the history of success and dissemination of computer technologies. It is rooted in the quite mythical character of the term "digital". As a mythical term, "digital" carries with it claims—hopes as well as fears—which suggest that it might have something "up its sleeve" since it is, in the spirit of Roland Barthes' understanding of mythology, a historical form and a way of signifying.

Since the end of the 1980s at the latest, the word "digital" has been so charged with associations perceived as both promises of salvation and threats of disaster that its every use leads to the proliferation of such associations. This applies to claims expressed by the adjective (digital revolution/era/world etc.) and the noun (digitalisation, digitality) as well as to any mythological analysis of the term "digital".

It is precisely in opposition to this that the neologism "digitalicity" intervenes (Holert 2002; Distelmeyer 2017, pp. 98–113). As an unwieldy speech act of despair, digitalicity is meant to give voice to the mythical concept of the digital, which more pre-describes than describes, without reproducing its mythical dimension. The power of mythical terms is that they produce what they supposedly only represent. Digitalicity, on the other hand, allows us to explicitly address the connotation of "digital" that is otherwise implicit and seems almost natural.

Critique of mythical attributions has been a growing part of discourses since the 1990s, which I will refer to continually in the further course of this chapter. The familiar associations of "digital" involving freedom, empowerment, control and participation and, time and again, flexibility and immateriality have been repeatedly revisited, discussed and critiqued. The era of a radiant optimism, exemplified by Nicolas Negroponte as the academic figurehead of digitalicity in the 1980s and '90s, seems to be over, especially since the mid-2010s. "[M]y optimism comes from the empowering nature of being digital," Negroponte (1995a, p. 230) emphasised at the time in his bestseller *Being Digital*, specifying this empowerment as "the access, the mobility, and the ability to effect change".

But that is history. For public scepticism towards digitalicity has been on the rise, especially since Edward Snowden's revelations in 2013 about the NSA's surveillance practices, and the subsequent scandals concerning data abuse and leaks on platforms such as Facebook. Put into sharp focus here are not only the conditions but crucially also the consequences of interconnectedness, ranging from the "like economy" (Gerlitz and Helmond 2013) of a computer-based and computer-induced "culture of connectivity" (Dijck and José. 2013) and the "dangers [...] of the monopolistic ambitions of global corporations and mass surveillance" (Schulz 2015, p. 9), to debates on fake news and post-truth (cf. Pourghomi et al. 2017; Bucher 2018, pp. 118–148). Thus the internet is becoming a problem for the very same promises of empowerment and freedom in being digital that have gained huge momentum through its use since the 1990s.

Criticism of the internet's development and of phenomena such as "echo chambers" in which "groups of like-minded individuals, consciously or not, avoid debate with their cultural or political adversaries" (Lovink 2012, p. 2) was followed by some radical advice. In 2018, for example, Jaron Lanier's book *Ten Arguments for Deleting Your Social Media Accounts Right Now* became a bestseller, with its meaty sentiments such as "social media is making you into an asshole" (Lanier 2018, p. 39), while

1.2 Myth/Matter (Digitalicity and Computerisation)

in 2019, Evgeny Morozov (2019, p. 17) summarised "digital resistance" as follows: "The observation that the 'techlash'—our so-called rude awakening to the gargantuan power of tech companies—is gaining strength with every month that passes, is already an obvious truth."

Nevertheless, the mythical aspects of digitalicity are still potent and valid, using the adjective "digital" in a "diffuse way to mean 'new', 'progressive' and 'computer-technical'"(Schröter 2004, p. 7) while at the same time addressing "notions of feasibility and controllability" (Holert 2002). More than ever, progress is digital: The urgency of "digitalisation" has become the new driving force of digitalicity.

During the 2017 federal election campaign in Germany, this urgency was reflected in the appropriately blunt advertising slogan "Digital First, Concerns Second" (FDP 2017, p. 3). It was precisely this invocation of digitalicity, in which everything is staked upon the recognition of its urgency, that showed what has changed in the process, namely that now "concerns"—here, clearly, old-fashioned hesitancy—are even surfacing where the magic word "digital" should automatically displace such obstructions.

This perspective was reinforced by the COVID-19 crisis, which saw private and professional communication alike forcibly shut down in the spring of 2020 and online communication taking their place. It makes "worriers look old" (Meyer 2020) because "[t]he digital, ostracised by cultural pessimists and progress skeptics as a harbour of human alienation, in fact sustains work processes, opportunities for learning, and crucially social interaction." (Rosenfeld 2020).

Exactly 13 months after Morozov's statement on the techlash, Deepti Bharthur of the Indian NGO "IT for Change" had to acknowledge that actually the opposite tendency was true. After 2019, "the year of 'the first great big techlash'", the COVID-19 lockdown had given "Silicon Valley and its counterparts around the world" (Bharthur 2020) the opportunity for new markets, new significance and a new reputation. The increasing relevance of the online offerings of "digital corporations"—from social media and news portals, to internet commerce, internet services and video conferencing technologies, which facilitated not only a new kind of private communication but above all possibility to work from home for millions of people—increased their importance for the global economy and portrayed "digital economy players" in a better light, "away from the regulatory din that has surrounded them for some time" (ibid.).

A new certainty: The thesis that "digitalisation [...] is above all a question of acceptance" and that "little encourages acceptance as much as the corona crisis" (Müller 2020, p. 77) was also echoed by the German Minister of State for Digitalisation. According to Dorothee Bär, this was "an initial spark" for digitalisation—even if it was "regrettable that it should take a crisis in our own country to make us rethink digitalisation, to overcome any remaining reservations and to see its inherent opportunities for improving lives" (Bär 2020).

The term "digital" therefore remains mythical the more hopes and fears are associated with it and layered onto it. Improvements such as "barrier-free digital administrative procedures that are geared to the living conditions of citizens and the needs of the economy and not just to the jurisdiction of authorities" (Bundesregierung 2014, p. 40) are mentioned in the same breath as criticisms of the influence and tax avoidance strategies of "digital corporations such as Google, Apple or Facebook" (Mussler 2017).

The pressure of urgency, however, is much more evident than any techlash. This side of digitalicity, significantly reinforced by the COVID-19 pandemic, boils down to inevitability. "[W]hether or not we want digitalisation is no longer the relevant question" (Schulz 2015, p. 11), but rather digitalisation as both the present and the future, as both the shared hope and—precisely for that same reason—the shared concern. For a welcome consequence of this urgency is that it creates a "we" united by the normalising relevance of digitalisation. National economies, societies, political parties and businesses face the question of whether and indeed how "we" can keep up.

This urgency is expressed through the certainty with which, for example, governments see "digital infrastructure" (Obama 2009, pp. 731–735) and the "shaping of digital change" (Bundesregierung

1.2 Myth/Matter (Digitalicity and Computerisation)

2018, p. 4) as defining the present regardless or without any doubt, and with which "digital convergence" is seen as "essential for Germany's prosperity" (Oberndörfer 2018). The future will have been digital. Thus the question of whether it is even possible to think about technologies today without assuming the dominance of digitality and networks may indeed be almost a rhetorical one (cf. Galloway and Leeker 2017, pp. 63–64).

What is pressing here as a kind of Future-II-Logic was already described by Florian Rötzer as "ideology of the information society" years before Negroponte's *Being Digital* (Rötzer 1991, p. 25). Rötzer's description at the beginning of the 1990s reads like a commentary on the urgency gesture of digitalicity three decades later:

> It is a question, as per the usual jargon of progress ideology, of not just missing the connection to the future but at the same time meeting the challenges of technological change. The logic of behaviour propagated in this context is one of a forced lack of alternatives. (ibid., p. 10).

The neologism of digitalicity is intended to address this sense of urgency without automatically reinforcing it. It responds to the status of the digital as a new condition of nature, a concept already formulated by Negroponte and which gained explosive momentum in the 2010s to the point where "digitalisation is portrayed by journalistic coverage as something quasi-natural" (Arlt et al. 2017, p. 95). In light of this mythical energy, digitalisation can seem like a new form of benevolent power. Like divine omnipresence it is with us at night and in the morning, and certainly on every future day.

Such a dream of boundlessness—which Wendy Chun (2013, p. 115) has described as "something close to universality, that is, digitality"—is realised through concepts such as the "technosphere" (Schneider 2019) and "technoecology", in which technology is equated with computer technology, and which, through the effects of autonomisation, brings about almost literally an "explosion of agencies" (Hörl 2016, p. 44). In technical and material terms, it is being pursued in particular alongside the expansion of internet infrastructures and the new 5G mobile communications standard as a "key technology for the realisation of digital transformation" and its "unprecedented requirements in terms of connectivity, capacity, security and performance" (BMVI 2017, p. 2).

This results in the challenging situation that "digital transformation" is both a mythical quantity and a material reality. Indeed, myths are always an effective part of reality. However, in the case of computerisation—a more fitting word for the comprehensive reliance on computer technology and computer logic—the momentous mythical and discursive along with the equally momentous technical and material aspects of digitality at once come into existence. They quite simply belong together.

How they interact is also a question of speed. The pace of both technical advances and the thrusts of innovation show themselves in the form of the speed at which I, as a "user" and part of the "digital era", am called upon to update, continuously and permanently. "Things and humans that are not updated are things and humans that are lost, out of date or in trouble, for we too have become updatable beings", writes Wendy Chun (2016, p. 2). Commenting further with Ursula Frohne on this imposition of constantly being up-to-date, she continues: "To be is to be updated: To update and to be subjected to the update."

Although the tangibly increasing pressure for progress is a phenomenon that has been recognised since the eighteenth century, it is precisely here that the specific nature of computerised progress lies: In the very programmability that makes the dogma of updating possibly in the first place.

Programmability has been described by biologist and computer scientist Michael Conrad (1988, p. 286) as the ability to "prescriptively communicate a program to a real-time system". The form of such a programme, however—a "rule that generates the behavior of a system" (ibid., p. 287)—and the framework of this prescriptiveness is bound in computers themselves to the strict formalism of computability and to "a finite set of primitive operations and symbols" (ibid., p. 288). Only what can be expressed and displayed within the framework of this formalism can become part of the computations of restricted relations. This is the "price of programmability" within the "theoretical limits of information processing" (Heilmann 2018, p. 176).

1.2 Myth/Matter (Digitalicity and Computerisation)

On this basis, computers remain flexible. They have the status of being general purpose machines and can fulfil any (though not all) purpose by being programmed to fulfil *specific* purposes over and over again. All purposes that can somehow be brought into being by the computing power of a computer can therefore be fulfilled by other computers because its only fixed purpose is precisely that of computing (cf. Coy 1994, p. 19). Put more precisely: This multiplicity of purposes exists because, and insofar as, they can be processed by the means of a computing machine that performs computation as a rule-based manipulation of signs.

Thanks to precise, decisive sequences of algorithmic chains of commands that follow "if/then" decision logic, these indeterminate machines can be determined. Again and again. This is what defines the "programmable purpose" (ibid.) of these machines: Their literally *decisive programmability*.

For this reason, computers are linked to a unique assurance of innovation in the forms of boundless progress and built-in potential for improvement, as reflected in the remarkable ambition of "new media" to establish super-temporal relevance with perpetual change as part of their very name. New never gets old. This form of *being* is designed to look towards *becoming* different. Thus, computers could indeed become the ideal machines and effectors of such social changes discussed as "flexible capitalism", "new spirit of capitalism" and "invocations of neoliberalism" (cf. Distelmeyer 2012, pp. 217–239).

This makes engaging with digitality all the more complicated. For digitality itself is the challenge, simultaneously present in the reciprocal relationship between myth and material. Digitality can neither be achieved nor negotiated without digitalicity and its imperative urgency, while at the same time, discursive assumptions are superseded and thereby dragged along by profoundly material and far-reaching processes. This is why we can never speak only of the mythical, and never only of digitalicity.

To escape this conceptual pitfall at least partially, in what follows I will address the comprehensive progression of "digitalisation" as *computerisation:* As both a material and ideological development. Myths with matter.

1.3 Discourse (Indefinite Definition)

The complexity of phenomena that are simultaneously mythical and material is further reflected in the use of the term digitality in media studies and other related disciplines. What is most striking in this case is how different the approaches are, with digitality proving to be an exceedingly inconsistent quantity, an indefinite definition.

Irrespective or not of whether such a divergence is at all "useful" because "different conceptualisations and methods may correspond to different phenomena of digitality in the object realm" (Schröter 2016), the difference of both meanings and approaches—and here we arrive at the third imposition and challenge of digitality—requires that we find a way to relate to these divergent positions. So the question arises once again: What is this digitality?

Explanations range from more technical constellations understood as "the synergy of circuit algebra, information, feedback plus electricity" (Mayer 2018, p. 42), and the media philosophical determination of "discretisation" (Krämer 2018, p. 54), to "the circumstance of living in a digital world, characterized by the proliferation and use of digital technologies" (Bennett 2014, p. 233). As an open, negotiable term, digitality is used primarily in the humanities—as a contrast to catchphrases such as digital transformation, digitalisation or digital revolution—although this antonym is hardly less problematic and overwhelming. By way of example, Robert Hassan (2020, pp. 1–2) describes digitality as "a humanist understanding of the processes of a machine, a logic, that has not only rapidly colonised every part of the inhabited planet, but has also suffused the consciousness of almost every person within it in terms of his or her engagement with each other through networks of communication, production and consumption". For Frieder Nake (2021/2016, p. 132), digitality is very much a thought construct, a "mental concept". As a concept, for Sean Cubitt (2016, p. 267) "defining the digital is as messy as the digital itself".

1.3 Discourse (Indefinite Definition)

Seb Franklin's (2015, p. xix) understanding is that "digitality [...] comes to describe not only a set of technologies or logical operations but also a fundamental condition". For him, digitality thereby evolves into a set of generalised metaphors and assurances of technical agencies which include in particular "their purported immateriality, flexibility, and freedom" (ibid., p. 6). Digitality offers the promise "to render the world legible, recordable, and knowable via particular numeric and linguistic constructs" (ibid., p. xix).

It is precisely the connotations of flexibility and immateriality cited above by Franklin—two enduring themes of digitalicity—that still now continue to play an essential role in the discussion of digitality. Nicolas Negroponte's famous 1995 proposition that "the digital world" is "much more flexible than the analog realm" was already aimed at overcoming material boundaries (1995b, p. 58). His suggestion that the "benefits and consequences of digital life" could be "best illustrated by observing closely the difference between atoms and bits" (ibid., p. 19) embedded the promise of immateriality in the game of digitalicity in a fundamental way.

This implicit flexibility, which Lev Manovich (2001, pp. 36–45) defined as variability and one of the five fundamental "principles of new media", is causally related to what is understood here as immateriality. For, as all processes in electronic digital computers are based on the sending of signals as states of electrical voltage, they are flexible, making any operation and thereby also the character strings, communications and commands based on them arbitrarily manipulable and transmissible. In short, computers offer flexible controllability, which is why they are so attractive to the concept of an adaptive governance of potentially anything.

Thus, for Negroponte (1995b, p. 47) digitality overcomes "the tyranny of space [...] and to some extent of time", and so on the profoundly material basis of directing electric charge, bits are said to conquer atoms. Physics beats physics.

The (post)operaist concept of "immaterial labour" joins in at this point insofar as it is intended to emphasise "the new quality of labor that produces the informational and cultural dimension of the commodity" (Lazzarato 1998, p. 39), which is inconceivable without the widespread use and interconnectivity of computers: Bodies are still working with matter. However, the adjective "immaterial" is intended here to underline the computer's contribution to these forms of work as well as the corresponding observation that such activities are not always recognised as work.

Notions of flexibility and immateriality have been determining factors in the discourse of digitality since the 1990s as the "shape-shifting openness of digitality" (Tholen 2002, p. 52), the "trend of immaterialisation" (Nake 2021/2009, p. 334), as "digital (virtual) ghost into the electronic computing machine" (Boast 2017, p. 15), the "immateriality of the digital itself" (Hayward 2013, pp. 107–108), and even as the very "dream of digitality: That you are matter-free" (King and Longo 2015, p. 96), the wide-ranging effectiveness of these notions being demonstrated in no small way by their global dissemination.

Dal Yong Jin (2015, p. 67) has argued that computerisation—as a phenomenon of globalisation "negotiated between *global forms and local materials*" (Ritzer 2018, p. 6) —is a new form of imperialism. What is being proliferated is by no means only hardware, software, and the platforms realised through them, but also ways of thinking and speaking about them.

Digitality, flexibility, and immateriality repeatedly converge, as Brazilian artist Fabíola M. Ribeiro and theorist Rejane Spitz illustrate in their explorations of the relationship between computers and art. With reference to projects by the Archigram Group from the 1960s, Ribeiro and Spitz (2006, p. 30) outline what constitutes "digitality" today in "our intensely, inescapably digital lives", i.e. "some sort of dematerialisation" in which "digital logic" is coupled with being "manipulable, flexible" (ibid., p. 24).

In their examination of economic developments in South Korea and China since 2009, Changwook Kim, Jack Linchuan Qiu, and Yeran Kim discuss digitalisation concerning both flexibility and immaterialisation. Addressing "Korea's cultural industry" (Kim 2018, p. 164) and the question of "how Korea and China responded to the 2008–2009 global economic crisis" (Qiu and Kim 2010, p. 630), they underline the extent to which the East Asian region has seen the development of a "digitized flexible production regime" (Kim 2018, p. 169) and "digital capitalism" (Qiu and

1.3 Discourse (Indefinite Definition)

Kim 2010, p. 645) which are linked to the processes of making flexible and immaterial, certainly regarding labour. "Both the positive and critical senses of immaterial labor" (ibid, p. 634) have rapidly become more important especially in South Korea and China (Kim 2018, p. 167).

Two distinctions need to be made at this point, as the dissemination of certain hegemonic belief systems and their related questions—which, for example, act as part of the platform imperialism described by Dal Yong Jin—may at first glance obscure non-Western traditions of thought. However it does not erase them. Rather, what is permanently at work here—and research from the 2010s in particular would appear to emphasise this—is amalgamation and appropriation, concepts that run both alongside and with one another.

With questions such as "how Asia-as-technê could become so easily adapted to our contemporary computational landscape", R. John Williams (2014, p. 215) has explored Asian influences on Western advanced technology and their related patterns of desire. In a similar vein, Matteo Pasquinelli has emphasised the significance of Hinduism and its rituals for the relationship between numbers, data, and algorithms that is immensely important today, especially regarding the development of machine learning: "Algorithmic processes encoded into social practices and rituals were that made numbers and numerical technologies emerge, not the other way around" (Pasquinelli 2019). In his reconstruction of technological thought in China, Yuk Hui (2016b, pp. 307–308) has discussed the "Qi-Dao relations" at work within it in order to make new technological futures and the "reappropriation of modern technologies" conceivable by leaning towards other epistemologies.

The second distinction concerns the concrete form which the dissemination of dominant belief systems and discourses takes. For although the connection between flexibilisation and digitalisation clearly both exists in and is discussed across an international space, it says little about respective positions towards this phenomenon.

The developments in Taiwan are particularly interesting for the dovetailing of theory and practice. Hopes for democratisation and participatory empowerment, especially in the 2000s, that accompanied the expansion of the internet in both Europe and the USA—and that have furthermore shaped its associated digitalicity—are in the process of entering a new and higher level. This process is made all the more interesting by contrasting developments in neighbouring China, where computerisation is being upscaled to new forms of social surveillance, assessment and control, and where the state plans to channel its population through a form of personal, social credit system using Big Data applications.

However, what easily gets obscured in this juxtaposition of Chinese "totalitarianism in digital disguise" (Strittmatter 2018, p. 12) and Taiwan's combination of democracy and computerisation are the following: Firstly, underlying connections that also affect Western democracies (cf. Wong and Dobson 2019; Ohlberg 2019), and not only because the Chinese "idea of a credit rating system is at least partly inspired by credit reporting services such as Schufa in Germany and FICO in the US" (Ohlberg 2019, p. 61). This development in China can indeed be described as an intensification of platform cultures and structures, to which I will return later with concepts such as capture capitalism and affective computing.

Secondly, any such clear comparison is further undermined by country-specific procedures, as reactions to the 2020 COVID-19 pandemic have shown. Taiwan, along with China, was among the countries that used state tracking of mobile phones to monitor whether its citizens were complying with quarantine obligations. Unlike China, however, the Taiwanese government emphasised the exceptional nature of its mobile phone tracking, which was "minimized in necessary extent" in order to preserve "the protection of personal information and privacy" (Tang 2020, p. 2). The name for this demonstratively flexible control fits perfectly with the mythical immateriality of the boundaries it has thus maintained: "Digital Fence" (ibid).

In Taiwan, Digital Minister Audrey Tang is driving this initiative, promoting "a collaborative ecosystem" in which "the government, the tech community and companies" work together to demonstrate that "code can support democratic values in a way

1.3 Discourse (Indefinite Definition)

that wasn't previously possible"(Tang 2019). The various platforms established by the government alongside civic hacker group g0v for petitioning and debating thus seem to promise a different kind of flexibilisation: A form of government that would itself become flexible insofar as it enables people to "exert their civic rights by making political decisions, as an outcome of a deliberative democracy" (de Vaujany et al. 2019, p. 14).

Achille Mbembe (2017, p. 3) also connects "flexible" and "digital" closely. In *Critique of Black Reason* "electronic and digital technologies" play a key role, leading Mbembe (2015, p. 33) to assert the provocatively essentialist thesis of a fundamentally digital continent: "Africa was digital before the digital". Justifying why he sees Africa as "fertile ground for new digital technologies" with what he calls "the spirit of the digital", he (2015, pp. 32–33) continues:

> [T]he philosophy of those technologies is more or less exactly the same as ancient African philosophies. This archive of permanent transformation, mutation, conversion and circulation is an essential dimension of what we can call African culture. [...] This flexibility and this capacity for constant innovation, extension of the possible, that is also the spirit of the Internet, it is the spirit of the digital, and it is the same spirit you will find in pre-colonial and contemporary Africa.

In this sense, Mbembe (2017, pp. 5–6) speaks of the "Becoming Black of the world". At a time when humanity is transforming "into animate things made up of coded digital data", the term "Black" refers for the first time not "only to the condition imposed on peoples of African origin (different forms of depredation, dispossession of all power of self-determination, and, most of all, dispossession of the future and of time, the two matrices of the possible)" (ibid.). From now on this dissolution of self-determination in favour of a flexible utilisation of individuals/data would be a new, worldwide form of existence.

The references to flexibility and immateriality are, as Mbembe's approach shows particularly clearly, by no means merely affirmative. Since the end of the 1990s, the emphasis has been growing on the materiality of this supposedly immaterial revolution, at first sporadically and from the 2010s increasingly markedly. As early as 1993, Friedrich Kittler's dictum "[t]here is no software" was probably the best-known opposition in German-language media studies to the disregard of hardware, to the gesture of the immaterial, and to the triumphal march of the software industry. What is crucial here is that Kittler understands programmability as "an attribute of hardware, not of software" (Heilmann 2018, p. 171); it is thus grounded in the "physicalised material structure of a computer (though this structure can be realised using different components, for example by electron tubes just as much as transistors or integrated circuits)" (ibid.).

In the context of debates on the Anthropocene (cf. Renn and Scherer 2015), the material turn, the geology of media (cf. Parikka 2015), and the orientation to "dealing calmly and straightforwardly with the seamless fabric of what I shall call 'nature-culture'"(Latour 1993, p. 7), in the twenty-first century theoretical and especially artistic responses to the myths of digitalicity increasingly emphasise material conditions and outcomes (cf. Lutz et al. 2015; Franke et al. 2016; Moll 2018; Andersen and Pold 2018, pp. 221–155). Furthermore, there is a growing debate around the "myth of immateriality" (Paul 2007, p. 269), the "myth of disembodiment in the digital" (Robben 2012, p. 20), and the "material representation of the internet [...] blurred in the social imagination" (Moll 2018).

The underlying factors of cables, server parks, processual infrastructures, bodies and machines, scandalous working conditions that form part of the mining, recovery and recycling of necessary raw materials, computer debris, and not least energy consumption for computer usage, are all thus brought to the surface.

The data traffic of the internet alone, to which permanently online, connected smartphones contribute increasingly, is growing into a crucial factor in the consumption of energy and the resulting environmental impact on the planet. Represented in CO_2 equivalents, the energy demand of data centres in Germany in 2018 was already "roughly equivalent to CO_2 emissions caused by air traffic in Germany" (Eckert 2018). For many years, the subjects of artist Joana Moll's projects have been the negotiation of the internet's materiality and the relationship between digitality and energy consumption (cf. Moll 2022).

According to Greenpeace research, if the internet were a country, it would already be ranked sixth among the world's nations with the highest energy consumption in 2017 (Weiland 2017). In the same analysis, the energy consumption of the global IT industry—i.e. the entire sectors of development and maintenance as well as usage of computer systems, software and networks—came in third behind China and the USA (Cook 2017, p. 16). The trend, just like the temperature of the world's climate, is rising: By approximately 9% annually (TSP 2019, p. 15).

Thus, as is becoming more apparent, the technology that is supposed to deliver the long-standing promises of immaterial flexibility and empowerment is actually expanding into and through the very opposite of these hopes. Computerisation is made reality through an exploitation that touches more than the issues of energy resources and raw materials (cf. Franklin 2015, p. 6). Working and living conditions are also affected, both of those who carry out piecework with computers as clickworkers and of those who are involved in the production and scrapping of devices.

Interconnections are laid out (cf. Mantz 2008; Qiu 2012; Heilmann 2015; Wan 2019) and rendered visible, audible and re-playable through, for example, the computer game *Phone Story* (Molleindustria, 2011) and the desktop documentary *All That Is Solid* (Louis Henderson, 2014). All this is played out on the very devices that result from either the enslavement and child labour that take place in the Congo for the extraction of coltan ore—the raw material necessary for the construction of computer hardware —or the (self-) murderous working conditions in Shenzhen, China, under which devices are manufactured there, or the work carried out at the electronic waste dumps in Ghana, Pakistan or China, where residual metals are melted out of the scrapped computers with almost no protection for the workers (cf. Fig. 1.1).

Growing attention towards the material conditions of computer technology, its propagation, interconnectedness and its quasi-autonomy understandably leaves its own mark on the very definition of digitality. "The digital materializes in a wealth of

Fig. 1.1 Screenshot from the fourth level of the computer game *Phone Story* (Molleindustria, 2011), in which players oversee the recycling of eWaste, a process harmful to health and the environment, thus simulating and experiencing a small share of the working conditions related to the devices they are holding in their hands while playing

forms: electricity, light, punched tape, radio signals," Sean Cubitt (2016, p. 267) asserts, highlighting yet another function of electricity. For it is its "magic" that helps the immaterial character of digitalicity to unfold both historically and ideologically: "[T]he digital is clean: smooth, depthless, immaterial".

Cubitt importantly observes that digitality inherited its supposed cleanliness and purity from the commercialisation of electricity at the beginning of the twentieth century, "a period when the production of energy was for the first time dissociated from its consumption" (ibid., p. 266). This inheritance cannot be separated—and it is worth remembering that "[c]leanliness is always a matter of moving the dirt elsewhere"—from the dynamic complex upon which digitality is also based: Namely, a space-consuming and persistently processual infrastructure of energy production, material extraction, and human and planetary exploitation that is itself part of the "physical weight of digital media" (ibid.). The lightness of the digital weighs heavily, its cleanliness is dirty.

1.4 Friendly Takeover (the Net)

The alleged purity of the digital nourishes its mythical potential. Untainted by matter, the magic of the digital is designed to unfold, its ideological persuasiveness *and* technical contingencies intimately entwined with those of electricity. Here "the magic of electricity" is at work, which—for his Victorian audience—may have made its researching physicist William Thomson (alias Lord Kelvin) "probably the most respected shaman of his time" (Lahiri Choudhury 2010, p. 124). It is noteworthy that Thomson went on to apply his research to the transatlantic telegraph link, which as recently as 1925 had been described as a fusion of magic and mystery: "It combines with the magic of electricity the tang and mystery of the sea." (Gray 1925, p. 48).

The second chapter of this book will consider the significance such references to telegraphy and electricity might have for a critique of digitality. And it will bring to the fore questions concerning *interface* layers and processes of *leiten* to develop the suggestion of using interface analyses as a concrete starting point for a critique of digitality.

Before we arrive there, however, there is a further connection between digitality and telegraphy that requires discussion. It concerns an important progression in the discourse with which the (determinably indeterminate) boundaries of digitality become shaped by a fourth imposition and challenge. For in the 2010s, its meaning shifted noticeably: Digitality and connectivity are now one.

To this effect Felix Stalder, whose German essay *Kultur der Digitalität* (2016) was translated as *The Digital Condition* in 2017, maps out an exemplary conclusion drawn from the critique of immateriality, and the simultaneity of computerisation's mythical and material phenomena. Crucially Stalder (2017, p. 9) refuses to distinguish "between 'digital' and 'analog,' 'material' and 'immaterial'", since even "in the digital condition, the analog has not gone away", but is "re-revalued and even partially upgraded". In a way similar to the ongoing proliferation and intensification of immaterial work with computers, factory jobs "have not simply disappeared; they have just been partially relocated outside of Western economies" (ibid., p. 18).

Stalder confronts the first imposition of digitality, its first challenge, by attempting to break down the various facets of its totality. In doing so, the "changes in the labor market", the "self-empowerment of marginalized groups" and the "dissolution of the centralized culture geography" all come into view, as do the expansion of the fields of culture, the growing importance of complex technologies as the basis of everyday life and "the development of the internet as a mass medium" (ibid., p. 5).

Opting for the double singular "culture of digitality" in the German essay—despite such emphatically diverse forms and consequences of computerisation—can be seen not just as a response to it, and its assumptive behaviour and logic, but also as an echo of its sense of urgency. The singular noun "digitality" indicates that its decoded constituent parts are all conditioned and motivated by the same technology, while the singular noun "culture" speaks of the fact that for Stalder (2016, pp. 9–10) these processes—which initially ran parallel to and yet independently of one another and as such were potentially reversible—are today intimately "intertwined and socially dominant as a coherent culture of digitality".

Stalder's definition of digitality is derived from this and testifies to the paradigm shift now taking place:

> 'Digitality' thus denotes the set of relations that is currently being realised based on the infrastructure of digital networks in the production, implementation and transformation of material and immaterial goods, as well as in the configuration and coordination of personal and collective action. (ibid., p. 14).

1.4 Friendly Takeover (the Net)

Digitality is based on the net. The internet and its "expansion at the turn of the millennium into a ubiquitous communication and coordination infrastructure" (ibid., p. 73) are, according to this logic, not simply manifestations, forms or intensifications of digitality. Protocol-based networking (cf. Galloway 2004)—which is in fact a particular articulation of the larger context of the conditions and effects of electronic digital computers—now becomes its new foundation: The digital is the networked.

This new equation is similarly employed in Yuk Hui's significant research of digital objects. As digital objects, Hui (2016a, pp. 1–2) examines the data sets and types that become unified objects and come to us, for example, as "online videos, images, text files" or as profiles on Facebook: "[D]ata and metadata, which embody the objects with which we are interacting, and with which machines are simultaneously operating" (ibid., p. 48). "Digital" here refers in particular to the recent development of networked computing, "that which we have since proclaimed as the digital" (ibid., p. 49), i.e. data exchange extending beyond individual computers, data networks between platforms.

Thus, the meaning of digitality shifts away from the totality and singularity of the action of diversifed computers and over to their interconnectedness as a new fundamental position. "The imperative to go online is spreading," asserts Dorle Dracklé (2014, p. 400), elaborating on the "normative instance" that "the internet, social networks, and smartphones" have become. Crucially even if this conclusion seems no less normative in this case, the imperative—also on the conceptual level—seems to be gaining widespread acceptance. The digital goes online.

Not only is the term "digital culture" in everyday life "nowadays frequently associated with the use of the internet and social media" (Ochsner 2016), but its definition in cultural studies as a "late-modern culture of digitality" (Reckwitz 2018, p. 243) also assumes that the formative factors of "algorithms" and "digitalisation" have meanwhile been reshaped by the "*communicative [] networking* between computers (as well as other apparatuses)" (ibid., pp. 231–232).

The same conceptual shift can be observed in sociology, as Philipp Staab's research on the platform economy and the proprietary markets of a few internet corporations demonstrates. For Staab (2019, pp. 12–14), "what is digital about digital capitalism" is precisely not "digital technology"; instead, its "gravitational centre" lies "in the commercial internet, whose leading companies have become the decisive interfaces for more and more economic processes and without which the omnipresent computers would only be simple calculating machines".

Governmental policy also operates repeatedly in the same manner with the digital. The German Federal Interior Minister's 2016 statement on data politics declared "data as the backbone of our digital present and future" because "networked electronic devices increasingly shape our everyday lives" (de Maizière 2016). In 2022, the German Federal Minister for Digital and Transport summarised: "The digitalisation is based on a global network" (Küpper 2022). The internet, it seems, defines digitality.

The debate about the importance of digital technologies in the face of the COVID-19 Crisis in 2020 introduces an existential dimension to this re-definition. Here, "digital" repeatedly means a state of programmatic interconnectedness. Here, "digital tools" are means of an "online culture" (Roose 2020). Here, "the natives of the digital age" are united by the experience of "how awesome, how helpful digital connectivity can be" (von Gehlen 2020), and nothing less than precisely "the digital" maintains and perpetuates "work processes, learning opportunities, and social interaction" (Rosenfeld 2020). Criticisms of increasing online commerce as an exacerbation of platform capitalism also place "digital infrastructures" as synonymous with internet infrastructures and services (Marx 2020). Just as the COVID-19 pandemic may have promoted acceptance of "digitalisation," it has further normalised the equation *digital = networked.*

The most paradoxical consequence of this development, however, can be found in the film industry. In order to advertise the exploitation of their products both through digital formats such as Blu-ray and DVD and through online availability via streaming and download all in one go, some subtle distinctions have been introduced. In addition to Blu-ray and DVD, films are now also available "digitally" (cf. Figs. 1.2 and 1.3.). The Digital Versatile Disc, once the technology whose digitality was so extensively

Fig. 1.2 Film advertising by Universal (Universal Pictures Home Entertainment 2019)

Fig. 1.3 Film advertising by Weltkino (Weltkino Filmverleih 2018)

advertised and promoted as a unique selling point from the mid-1990s, is no longer digital enough. Thus Amazon, as a streaming platform, was able to announce the exploitation of the series *You Are Wanted* with the absurd aside that soon "the series will also be available on DVD—completely analog" (Amazon 2017).

This everyday shift in the meaning of "digital", which goes far beyond academic conceptual work, in its own way sustains digitalicity's gesture of immateriality. The myth indeed lives on, however, not just through persistence, but through a shift that is at the same time an intensification.

Whereas in the 1990s "digital" was thought of as distinct from "analog" and as the dissolution of bulky matter in favour of a quasi-immaterial flexibility, along with its promise of interaction (digitalisation as transformation, i.e. "old" becomes "new"), the equation of "digital" and "networked" enshrines an already ongoing efficiency of exchange and transfer processes. *It's a kind of magic*. The running infrastructures, necessary resources, apparatuses and regulations that make such processes possible in the first place become even less visible when the outcomes of connectedness become synonymous with the very term that once claimed merely to denote the transition to a new technology. Furthermore when the term "digital" becomes synonymous with the performance of computer networks, with the protocological functionality of the internet, attention shifts further from material contingency and on to magical effectiveness.

In this way, contexts and dependencies are easily lost from view. This also applies to the historical dimension of the internet based on (not as an equivalent of) digital computer technology. Joseph Vogl (2021, p. 66) has emphasised in this regard that the geneology of the internet is precisely not a purely technical history and also does not go back "straight to a military-industrial institution under the sign of the Cold War", but must also be understood in connection with the genealogy of financial markets and stock exchange transactions, electronic trading systems and privatisation of information technology infrastructures.

Neither computers nor their networks can indeed be explained by hardware alone. Materiality is by no means the only thing able to reveal what digitality is. But even more than the functioning of my computer, which I can hold in my hands, network infrastructures such as undersea cables, radio networks and server parks are hidden from my view, thus bringing the sense of magical possibilities all the nearer.

The nebulous concept of *the cloud*, "today's dominant metaphor for digital space" (Hu 2015, p. 147), equally lends weight to

Fig. 1.4 Internet without computers: Screenshot from the Telekom commercial for the "Connecting Europe" campaign (Telekom 2016)

the "preferred image of the Internet" as "a sort of nebulous solar system, a cosmic 'cloud' "(Blum 2012, p. 16), as does the 2016 Europe campaign by German telecommunications company Telekom. In a commercial for the campaign entitled "Connecting Europe", singer Andrea Bocelli, who lost his eyesight at the age of 12, moves completely freely through a selection of European locations. As a result, the internet is literally advertised without a single glimpse of computers (of any kind) (cf. Fig. 1.4). Bocelli speaks—offstage, appropriately disembodied—of "the network" that transcends borders, the net that is both "indispensable and invisible" and "the present and the future," concluding by linking his own blindness to the immateriality of this technology with the commercial's final sentence: "You can't see it—but you can feel it." (Telecom 2016).

1.5 Critique ...

Critique is a constant, increasingly perceptible companion to the conditions and consequences of computer technology. All the aspects of digitality mentioned so far—and many more that arise from them, concerning dimensions not yet discussed—have already become the subject of various forms of critique.

From the very beginning. In 1950, only 4 years after the introduction of the first electronic digital computer ENIAC (Electronic Numerical Integrator and Computer), Norbert Wiener published his concerns in *The Human Use of Human Beings: Cybernetics and Society*. This objection is particularly noteworthy because it comes from Wiener himself.

The reason for this is that Wiener's concern "about uncontrolled commercial exploitation and other unforeseen consequences" (Brockman 2019, p. 11) referred to the same cybernetic "control technologies" for which his own and most famous paper from 1948, *Cybernetics: Or Control and Communication in the Animal and the Machine,* had established a crucial theoretical basis. Assumptions of cybernetics—not least the equation of the terms "communication" and "control" (Stalder 2016, p. 58)—guide the spread of computer technology to this day, something that is all too evident in the feedback principle of smart cities and smart homes.

In 1950, Wiener saw the danger in making exact and unnuanced decisions—as is the case with computer calculations of numerical data—the unquestioned basis of political and military action, and the risk of becoming, as he expressed in the words of Dominique Dubarle, a *"machine à gouverner"* (Wiener 1989, p. 179).

So, for Wiener these governing machines are dangerous not because they strive for or could achieve autonomous control and domination, as portrayed not long after in the 1957 Hollywood film *The Invisible Boy*, where a 4000 cubic metre-large supercomputer goes berserk. His critique is instead aimed at the fact that machines are being used by humans to control humanity, and that political leaders are developing techniques inspired by this machine-based model.

This expansion of statistics and precise calculations, which seizes all individuals and makes them equal (at least as far as calculability is concerned), has been portrayed by Wiener (ibid., p. 181) as a distant horror scenario: "Fortunately we have not yet reached such a state." Yet his portrayal is remarkably close to current computerisation scenarios, which involve progressive reliance on widespread, interconnected, and quasi-autonomous computers. The trend towards "anticipatory government" observed by Perricos and Kapur (2019, p. 41)—i.e. "predictive analytics and artificial intelligence (AI) [which] allow governments to target likely problems before they erupt into crises"—echoes Wiener's concerns, while for John Brockman "Wiener's warning cries are a reality today", and should be "reconsidered by researchers at the forefront of the AI revolution" (2019, p. 11). Furthermore Rouvroy and Berns' (2013) description of an "algorithmic governmentality" and Gabrys's (2016) analysis of "citizen sensing" reinforce the timeliness of Wiener's sentiments.

In her reflections on ubiquitous computing and smart cities Gabrys (2016, p. 18) emphasises in particular the function of the sensors used in this context: "technologies that make possible the distribution of computational logics beyond the screen and interface to spatial and environmental applications". Sensors gather and deliver input on the things they measure, and in combination with software developed for their task, create the world that they purport only to capture.

They provide for "automated sensing processes" in which patterns are detected and form the basis for taking action, thus turning computer technology into "seemingly autonomous agents", (ibid., p. 65). Thus Gabrys (2016, p. 328) shows how the actions of sensors and computers are involved in the production of not only new environments but crucially new forms of society, in which "a 'microphysics of power' is exercised and practiced in everyday scenarios" through a state of continuous surveillance.

The critique of algorithmic governmentality is likewise oriented towards questions of power. It concerns a specific type of automation achieved through the use of Big Data and machine learning. Antoinette Rouvroy's and Thomas Berns' assertion argues that both the power and the danger of making such statistical practices independent lie in a new, "(a) normative" indifference towards individuals. By repeatedly targeting and establishing relationalities, data-mining's automated procedures result in new forms of normativisation that essentially stem from the self-learning nature of these systems:

> [W]e would like to strongly emphasize this "algorithmic governance's" indifference to individuals, insofar as it simply focuses on and controls our "statistical doubles", in other words combinations of correlations, produced automatically and using big data, themselves constituted or collected "by default". In short, what we are, "roughly", to use Eric Schmidt's term, is precisely no longer ourselves (singular beings) in any way. (Rouvroy and Berns 2013, p. 180).

For Antoinette Rouvroy (2013, pp. 145–161), this type of data-mining-based governance, therefore, eludes classical forms of critique. Algorithmic governance—a development of the governing machine outlined by Norbert Wiener, but one using algorithmic decision-making—shapes the future automatically, as it were, without having to subject its plans to any tests. It can dispense with any engagement with its subjects since it operates "with infra-individual data and supra-individual patterns". It influences individuals and groups through "alerts or stimuli producing reflex responses rather than interpretation and reflection" (ibid., p. 155), thus bypassing the possibility of confrontational encounters with human subjects. In short, for Rouvroy, this automated logic of computerisation avoids the challenge of human freedom.

In contrast, Luciana Parisi (2017, pp. 75–100) hopes that "computational logic" (as it is developing) will provide a way out of this scenario. For her, the excessive demands that the unimaginable processes of machine learning place on humans could lead to a far-reaching and major crisis of human thought. This could challenge the prevailing image of technology that "machines are always already made in the image of man, and as such determine what the human subject is and does" (Parisi 2019, p. 30).

Thus Parisi seeks to use the very dynamics of this techno-logic—the software processes "in the networks of artificial intelligences that are constantly learning from each other" (ibid., p. 27)—to appeal against "technocapitalist governance" (Parisi 2017, p. 86). Along with the affront on humans through technology's excessive demands, "reasoning has become instrumental to the transformation of reasoning itself" and thus a (philosophical) escape from "the alienating condition of thinking with and through machines" becomes all the more urgent (Parisi 2019, p. 47).

1.5 Critique ...

While Rouvroy and Berns oppose automated computational logic, Parisi attempts to think with it in order to question established modes of thinking. Ten years earlier—i.e. at the point when the neural networks of machine learning started to attract sustained attention—Frieder Nake (2021/2009, p. 336) had already stressed that the problem lies in "the very thought that machines can think". Fundamental critique of mathematics' rules and relations, which all computer operations follow, is likewise emphatically opposed to the assimilation of computer logic.

In this sense, Sybille Krämer and Dieter Mersch trace digitality back to the fundamentals of the binary code with which computers work. Their critique of computerisation as an enforcing of "formalisation" (Krämer 2018, p. 40) intensifies Michael Conrad's assertion that the cost of programmability is the "basic problem of all programming" (Mersch 1991, p. 109) to the extent that it predicates "the reduction of reality into codable data." As programmes and programming languages can ultimately be described as "decision calculi"—on account of their "'if..., then...' logic processes"—computers can by definition be considered "decision-making machines". This means that all "problems" which use computers, in all their forms, for their solutions, must in turn be re-formulated into "decidable questions" (ibid., p. 111).

Heinz von Foerster (1993, p. 73), in discussing a second-order cybernetics and ethics, has stressed that "only *those* questions that are in principle undecidable can be decided by us. Why? Simply because the decidable questions are already decided by the choice of the framework in which they are posed, and by the choice of rules of how we connect what we call 'the question' with what we allow to be 'the answer'".

For Dieter Mersch (2019, pp. 68–69), this logic culminates in the enforcement of "algorithmic rationality", as if "the real were to be negotiated solely within the matrix of digitalism and its algorithmic networks, and were thus to be made subordinate to the perspectives of calculability and decidability, whose mathematical and universal embodiment, as we all know, is the Turing machine". In other words, as Seb Franklin (2015, pp. xix-xx) points out, for the promise of digitality to be fulfilled, and for it to be able to read, recognise, and digest the world with mathematical precision, the processes of capture, assessment, definition, optimisation, and filtering need to take effect. Thus before an event or object can be recorded and captured, what lays outside the parameters of the calculable is, as it were, automatically excluded. On this basis computers capture and convey the world.

The fact that the computer's claim to universality as a general-purpose machine becomes a somewhat tricky one is thus evident, and rooted in its computational procedures. As symbols of calculability, the "objects of the world, be they things or processes," will never enter the computer as "extended matter" through "the eye of the needle of input channels," but must allow themselves to be transformed "into signs" in order to then "become *initiators* of arbitrary internal algorithmic processes" (Nake 2021/2003, p. 313). For Mersch (2017), this is the basis of the "semblance of predictability" on which "governmental powers" rely, as do the "counter-strategies of subversive hacking", as if "everything were merely a question of the right algorithm".

Alexander Galloway's critique also starts with binarity and decision logic. Referring to Deleuze and Guattari, Galloway (2014) describes digitality as the oldest way of thinking and the oldest form of prejudice, since it requires deciding between two elements that are rigorously and consistently separated from each other. The principle of digitality therefore states that there is a suitable process of distinguishing for everything in the world, and it can occur between zeros and ones, "the binary mathematics driving modern computers" (ibid., p. xxxiii), as well as between two genders, between oneself and the other, between "us" and "them". It ultimately boils down to differentiation and decision.

The question of distinction and—no less importantly—similarities and correlations, occupies in a different way critical data studies, which emerged in the 2010s as a response to the hype around Big Data analyses. Added to a new divide between "the Big Data rich and the Big Data poor" to which Danah Boyd and Kate Crawford (2012, p. 674) subsequently drew attention, another fundamental problematic is gaining prominence. Wendy Chun's (2018, p. 76) objection to homophily as an axiom of network research is directed against the guiding assumption of Big Data analyses that "similarity breeds connection".

1.5 Critique ...

Networks of various types are at the centre of the current debate on digitality and computerisation including, for example, the Internet of Things as a "complex and capital-intensive ensemble of millions of servers interconnected by means of specialised software and, increasingly, custom-designed hardware" (Sprenger 2015, p. 41). In addition, Blockchain technology is a highly resource-intensive networking procedure involving a decentralised database, which is geared towards expansion and which promises new levels of security, autonomy and control (cf. Catlow et al. 2017). However, the greatest amount of attention remains focused on humans, and what in fact unites critique's different perspectives here is concern for the impact of computerisation on human subjects, groups, and indeed societies.

Forms of "digital control" are the focus of a critique of affective computing, referring to the "affect- and psycho-technologies" deployed in order to capture, store, measure, categorise, catalogue, operationalise, simulate, and induce affective states (Angerer and Bösel 2015, p. 48). Felix Maschewski and Anna Verena Nosthoff (2019, p. 58) have critiqued this "mode of socialisation" based on this as a "specific 'governmental programme'", using Facebook as one such example.

In doing so, they refer to the "cybernetic hypothesis" which, according to the Tiqqun collective (2020, p. 25), "would have us think of biological, physical, and social behaviours as being integrally programmed and reprogrammable". According to Maschewski and Nosthoff (2019, p. 73), the cybernetic hypothesis is substantiated through "Facebook's transformation of communication into an algorithmically readable operation"—i.e. formalised using decision logic, in that patterns of activity, habits and interests of "users" can be recorded, registered, catered for, "communicatively intensified and aligned in the character of a newsfeed". They cite as a concrete example (ibid., p. 56) the affair surrounding data analysis company Cambridge Analytica who, with the help of Facebook data, supported the 2016 Trump campaign in the run-up to the election of the 45th US president using programmatically personalised election advertising, which of course—and despite all the promised/feared effectiveness of digitality—could not itself decide the result of the election.

While the focus here is on issues of programming society through affective control and participation, the relationship between prescription and prejudice is about pre-existing influences. How social stereotypes find their way into programming.

Here, the critique is directed at algorithmically processed—and thus equally hidden and effective—clichées, as well as at "inscribed, encoded prejudices" (Bridle 2018, p. 142). Safiya Umoja Noble (2018, p. 1) speaks of "technological redlining" to show how implicit attributions related to "capital, race, and gender" influence the results of supposedly neutral computational processes and internet search queries: "On the Internet and in our everyday uses of technology, discrimination is also embedded in computer code and, increasingly, in artificial intelligence technologies that we are reliant on, by choice or not."

Against this background, James Bridle looks in particular at the training of artificial neural networks in machine learning processes. He confronts machine learning as a probabilistic technique of inferring the future from the past with Walter Benjamin's reflections on the concept of history: "[History] is never a document of culture without at the same time being one of barbarism" (Benjamin 2010, p. 34). Bridle (2018, p. 144) therefore critiques that the training and developing of "these nascent intelligences on the remnants of prior knowledge is thus to encode such barbarism into our future".

The exact opposite however is emphasised by Luciana Parisi (2018, p. 99). The AI learning processes behind this form of algorithmic decision-making—which operate using probability combined with trial-and-error—would mean in fact not "a design of the future by the past", but "an evolution of the past from the perspective of the future". For Parisi the future becomes yet another parameter as this type of machine learning not only recognises and learns patterns; on the contrary, it also learns the learning process itself, in that "the algorithms learn to modify their own paths through data searches" (ibid., p. 100). Therefore, the past, which can thus be recognised and become the further basis for forecasts and future decisions, is also grasped from a perspective of what is to come, insofar as the "automatic adaptation of results to rules" is at work in the process (ibid.).

1.5 Critique ...

Nevertheless, even Parisi's concern that ADM systems join and implement the present and the past as a probable future in no way cancels out Bridle's critique. Rather, both focus on different characteristics: Data used for training on the one hand, and processing modalities on the other. The compiled training data sets retain their conditional function, as does the commitment to the formalisation of decision-logic according to which patterns can be recognised; even "the smallest variations in context-specific content" can be captured and applied in terms of probability (ibid., p. 101). Machine learning, which works with iterative loops, is in fact both: It derives a probable past *and* future from patterns of previous data acquisition, and it processes the past from that computational perspective of "the future".

The question therefore remains how humans can follow and judge the criteria of such a "perspective", such "knowledge" and "learning" of this form of computerisation and thus the principles of its inherent momentum: The differences between Bridle and Parisi all point to this significant challenge for human thought.

Geert Lovink (2016, p. 7) has outlined further differences using a kind of continental schematic, charting various critical approaches to "internet theory" in recent years. On the one side, the "American approach, coming from Nicholas Carr, Andrew Keen and Jaron Lanier, who are primarily business writers, not academics—with the exception of Sherry Turkle—critiques social media for its superficiality". The group of European authors "such as Bernard Stiegler, Ippolita, Mark Fisher, Tiziana Terranova and Franco Berardi", and also Geert Lovink, forms the counterpart (ibid.). Their systematic critical project is described here as stressing "the wider economic and cultural context of (the crisis in) digital capitalism"—with the aim, emphasised by Lovink, to develop a new understanding of the internet and "of its functioning from the inside, as a technology, a *Kulturtechnik*, an industry and infrastructure of political economy" (ibid, p. 209).

Such groupings, although they offer clarity, always run the risk of simplification. What is added in the case of the continental context is the fact that a systematic critique in this second European sense has been developing and growing worldwide for some years, and it is directed against "capture capitalism" (Heilmann

2015) and "platform imperialism" (Jin 2015), "platform capitalism" (Srnicek 2017) and "surveillance capitalism" (Zuboff 2019). What is particularly salient here is the combining of processes of capturing with those of evaluation and control. As people interact with and are tracked, recorded and thus "sensed" by the digital technology of their devices (e.g. smartphones) and internet services (e.g. search engines), they consequently enter into new relations of value creation, exploitation and control.

For Shoshana Zuboff (2019, p. 255), the function of voice assistants such as Google Home and Amazon's Alexa consists above all in permanently evaluating human behaviour and placing it in the exploitative context of (market-relevant) predictions: "Unruly life is brought to heel, rendered as behavioral data and reimagined as a territory for browsing, searching, knowing, and modifying." What is referred to here as "surveillance capitalism," and which "transformed the web into a market onslaught fuelled by the capture and analysis of behavioural surplus" (ibid.), Till A. Heilmann calls capture capitalism.

"Capture" is understood by Heilmann (2015, p. 40) as "a technological-economic calculation designed to turn human actions as thoroughly as possible into data", which naturally includes more than one form of data accumulation. Just how "the 'whole human being' increasingly comes under the regime of informatic surveillance" when interacting "with personalized sensor technology such as electronic wristbands" is highly relevant here, as is the "strategic expansion of the zone of exploitation" represented by everyday human interaction with user interfaces on a variety of devices and platforms (ibid., pp. 44–45).

The concept of strategic expansion is taken up by Dal Yong Jin's (2015, p. 67) notion of platform imperialism, which refers to an asymmetrical relationship of interdependence between the West, in particular the USA, and many developing countries: "This includes the two great powers of nation-states and transnational corporations. But platform imperialism is not only about the forms of technological disparities but also the forms of intellectual property, symbolic hegemony, and user commodity".

The closeness of these three approaches to those of, for example, Gabrys, Chun, Mbembe, Berns, and Rouvroy reinforces the sense of transcontinental associations in terms of critique. For not only do the developments discussed here operate transnationally, but also the theoretical explorations and concerns, as was particularly evident in the 2018 article "Media, Communication and the Struggle for Social Progress", co-authored by 17 contributors from Australia, Canada, China, Colombia, Mexico, Russia, South Africa, South Korea, the United Kingdom, and the USA:

> It is a myth that rural communities, Indigenous peoples and the Global South are disinterested in media and the digital world, but our current media infrastructures carry little if any input from these large sections of humanity. What if media infrastructures and digital platforms were designed with communities' diverse languages, needs and resources in mind? (Couldry et al. 2018, p. 80).

They propose a ten-part action plan to address these issues practically ranging from the establishment of communication rights and "civil society participation in Internet and media infrastructure governance and policy" to "free access to software and free knowledge as the commons of humankind" (ibid., p. 83).

1.6   ... of Digitality (Unfolding Concerns)

That the impositions and challenges of digitality have had an impact on its very critique is undeniable. Furthermore the proliferation and diversification of the technology and ideology of "the digital" is reflected in the sheer diversity of reactions both have provoked, part of which I have only touched on here.

In German-language media studies in particular, numerous approaches have been explored in recent years to develop critical positions on tangible artefacts and processes of digitality and computerisation. For example, at the annual conference of the German Society for Media Studies (GfM) in 2016 more than 170 papers addressed the topic of "Critique", the "Programme of a Neo-Critical Media Studies" (Schröter and Heilmann 2016) was developed in Bonn, in Lüneburg the DFG Research Training Group "Cultures of Critique" was founded in 2016, and research groups within the Gesellschaft für Medienwissenschaft developed, among other things, strategies for a critique of data (cf. Gießmann and Burkhardt 2014) and of interfaces (cf. Wirth 2016a), which since 2018 has been a regular feature in the journal *Interface Critique*.

This is not to mention international developments in art, with its various forms of intervention in the field of digitality and in the "public debate and discourse on the rise of the data society and digital technologies" (Franke et al. 2016, p. 11), the sheer volume of which is impossible to survey. Not infrequently, however, works as well as both their creators and structures do indeed overlap with media studies discourses. Hito Steyerl and Trevor Paglen, Zac Blas and Joana Moll, Olia Lialina and James Bridle, the collectives Molleindustria and Agbogbloshie Makerspace Platform (AMP) are some such examples here along with Harun Farocki, whose influence continues to have an impact well beyond his death in 2014. They represent a movement that uses the media and materials of computerisation against itself.

Consequently, it is becoming increasingly clear that "the critique" of digitality is as elusive as "the digitalisation". Thus against a backdrop of the myriad critical approaches to the conditions, proliferation, embedding and quasi-autonomy of computer technology, what I am concerned with is the question of what can follow from this: with concrete proposals for a critique of digitality.

Those must start from the problems and obstacles that any such critique has to face, and the multitude of different processes that run under the mythical and magical word "digitalisation" cannot merely be appropriated and simplified into one single entity. The developments of user interfaces, for example, are different from those of machine learning. The social and political changes brought about by platforms such as Facebook and Twitter pose different questions than those concerning an 'Industry 4.0' conversion to automated production processes via computer networking of both plant technology and order management. The networking of schools means something different from the networking of refrigerators. At the same time, paradoxically, and despite all the differences and ramifications, a somewhat banal commonality must be pointed out: All these developments are

1.6 ... of Digitality (Unfolding Concerns)

based on the fact *that* computers and *how* computers are (further) developed.

It is by no means only equipment, programmes and infrastructures that are developed, in other words planned, brought into the world, constructed, organised and run. Guiding ideas are also developed. Ideas about what computers are and what humans are in relation to them, assumptions about the objectives of computerisation, beliefs in the importance of predictability, concepts of networks, notions of automation and autonomy, models of intelligence and learning.

Erich Hörl, Nelly Y. Pinkrah and Lotte Warnsholdt (2021, p. 7) have stressed that the "widespread implementation of computational media" poses a double challenge for a mode of critique: "it concerns the transcendental modality of critique, and on the other its practical modality". As important as this analytical distinction is, to emphasize not only the question of how critique can be thought at all here, but also that form of critique which proves itself in concrete dealings with what falls into the object field of critique, this must not be understood as a simplistic juxtaposition of theory and practice. Rather, what must be equally emphasized is the fact that the theoretical question of the (im)possibilities of critique that I am pursuing here, and as a result of which I will propose interface analyses as a practical modality (for which the concepts of *interface* and *leiten* play a key role), is itself a practice. And just as any transcendental modality of critique is a theoretical practice that works in a particular way with certain concepts and models, the foundations of non-human and "machinocentric and no longer logocentric" (ibid., p. 8) relations go back to human responsibility in the function of those programmatic machines, which in turn are developed in a particular way according to certain concepts and models.

This is also where the critique of cybernetics developed by Claus Pias sets in. Taking this "counter-science"—which had been able to "question human sciences", thereby escaping the "anthropological illusion"—Pias (2004, pp. 16–17) reconstructs it as an archaeology of ideas where it in turn only became successful by way of the "setting free of a cybernetic illusion". This cybernetic thinking drives (a particular development of) technology, calls "concrete interface design to task" (ibid., p. 26), and significantly shapes discussions concerning the connections "between technology and the social (under the rubric of catchphrases such as 'electronic government' or 'network society')" (ibid.).

Computerisation, which I understand to be a material and ideological development that relies on the power and logic of profoundly widespread, networked computers that are determined to be self-determining, is neither a unified process nor a set of disjointed paths of technological progress. This technology is not just any technology.

The *decisive programmability* of computers distinguishes these machines, in whatever forms they appear or are integrated, from all other machines. It distinguishes this technology from all other cultural, political, social or industrial technologies, with which computer technology (and its logic) is today nevertheless connected in both the broadest and most intrinsic way. Programmability, this highly specialised form of intended purpose, is thus also the foundation for the development of an "environmental constitutionality relating to media and technologies today" (Hörl 2018, p. 228), and is discussed as "techno-ecology", as a "shaking up and reordering" of the differences between nature and technology, and paradoxically as "absolutely beyond all purpose" (Hörl 2016, p. 44).

This is precisely why a critique of digitality is needed that is aware of this problematic and that is committed to investigating the diversity of forms and processes as well as the commonalities of their conditions. This requires an approach that overlooks as little as possible, and it must be as specific as it is open and scalable in order to be able to address this complexity and dynamic.

The project and scope of such a critique thus inevitably burden themselves with all the problems that make digitality an imposition: From the (over-)demanding multiplicity, presence and concealment of conditions, apparatuses and processes, through the interplay of mythical and material elements, and the differences and shifts in the understanding and use of the term digitality, right up to an equating of the "digital" and the "networked". A critique of digitality cannot circumvent any of these impositions. On the contrary, this is precisely where it must begin in order to develop as a concept, with its approach and key terminology, and in response to all these interrelationships. Staying with the trouble.

This of course places unique demands on the concept of a critique that attempts to do justice to both meanings of the term: Critique as debate and analysis, derived from the Greek κρίνειν (krínein) i.e. "to separate, judge, decide" (Röttgers 1975, p. 19), and critique as "a pronounced judgement in its own right" (Grimm and Grimm 1873). The two belong together. To critique without prior discussion and analysis must inevitably remain a kind of prejudicial judgment.

Michel Foucault, in a discussion with Didier Eribon in 1981, outlined how the two can come together thus:

> Critique does not mean merely saying that things are not good the way they are. Critique means identifying which insights, habits and acquired—but not reflected—ways of thinking the accepted practice is based upon. [...]Critique is the attempt to unearth this thinking and change it. It demonstrates that things are not as self-evident as one might think, so that they are no longer taken for granted. Critique means making things that come all too easily a little harder. Under such conditions, critique (and radical critique) is absolutely essential for change. (Foucault and Eribon 2005, pp. 221–222).

The question of what it is that an accepted practice is based on leads to conditions that go beyond cognition and ways of thinking, in terms of digitality and computerisation. The imposition of digitality reminds us of this: For a critique of digitality, to enquire about habits is equally to enquire about the material and programmatic conditions of established practices. It is true that infrastructures and machine processes are ever more closely linked to human activities, habits and ways of thinking, ranging from programming to the habitualised everyday and work use of commercially available computer formats, to being captured by the sensors of particular dynamic hardware-software configurations in, for example, "intelligent" street lamps that wait for our presence, or that are with us in our smartphones. Yet human modes of acting and thinking are not identical to computer processes.

In approaching this complexity of practice and habits we quickly near the limits of our own perception. What can I know about it and what can I observe? If "digital objects" such as YouTube videos are the materialised form of a set of metadata through which the "properties, functions, permissions of these objects, that in turn define the object's relations to other objects, as well as to the backend programme and to its users" (Hui 2015, p. 5), what else do I experience/understand about the existence of these objects? What do I know about digital voice assistants such as Siri, Alexa or Cortana? How can I understand what is going on in the neural networks of such software that record, analyse and process my speech input in order to refine the recognition of linguistic patterns and their associations?

To interrogate computerisation as a practice is to engage with the multiple intersections of human habits and computer-based processes. This is what constitutes (the imposition of) digitality. Without wishing to reinforce the "we" of digitalicity here or to level out the different conditions and relations under which people, wherever they may be, have to deal with the foundations, processes and consequences of computerisation, the Complex of digitality concerns us all because we belong to it.

I engage and participate on many levels. I buy or rent computers and actively use them. I am captured by sensory-enhanced computers. I have access to the very discourse of digitality—I have been taught what computers are, and I participate in this knowledge structure. I learn about and contribute myself to the manifold social, cultural, political, economic and ecological effects of computerisation. When researching the energy consumption data of internet usage, I use internet publications of research institutions. I am and remain involved.

Against this background of participation, it becomes important therefore to establish a critique, as Marina Garcés (2008) explains, that can no longer be conceived in terms of the maturity of a subject who is "capable of judgment". Instead,

> it is much more significant to have the courage to engage in a mode of existence that dares to be affected and exposed. It is no longer about the conquest of freedom as subjects move toward becoming independent from the world and others; it is now more about the conquest of freedom in our interlacements. (ibid.)

1.6 ... of Digitality (Unfolding Concerns)

In comparable ways, critique has been repeatedly linked to forms of participation in the recent past. This includes that form of self-participation also emphasised by Foucault as the relationship between critique and "self-forming" (Butler 2006): That is the need not to spare one's own "ways of thinking" (Foucault and Eribon 2005, p. 222) in the development of critique of an object field insofar as they are part of the "conditions by which the object field is constituted" (Butler 2006). Similarly, Sybille Krämer (2019, p. 37) has described critique as the willingness to "apply the standards of judging phenomena and utterances (also) to one's own thinking/doing".

The objective of a "de-automation" (Doll 2014, p. 246) of critique understood thus can also be attributed to Bruno Latour's both "a more critical consideration of ourselves in critical discourse" and "as an involvement in facts as [...] *things that concern us*" (Thiele 2015, p. 146). This self-involvement is (not only) linked to an additional, second form of involvement in Latour's case however. As is the case with other forms of critique, the object of this critique is, according to Latour (2004, p. 246), "fragile and thus in great need of care and caution". For critique here is something that does not end the discussion, rather it opens it up and offers "participants arenas in which to gather".

Using a similar metaphor, Antoinette Rouvroy (2013, p. 160) has proposed that a critique of algorithmic governmentality should "interrupt or grip the fluidity of our techno-capitalist reality" in order to generate "interstices". In these intermediate spaces, Rouvroy suggests, "the common may happen" insofar as individual and collective subjects gather jointly to find "new configurations between human existents, the law and technologies" (ibid., p. 162).

Therefore the critique that it is necessary to develop here should not be concerned with revealing an essential core. Its path is not one of the classical promise of an enlightenment that takes place through the lens of the distanced and judgmental critique's subject, uncovering the centre or essence of the critique's object. Beyond both the complexity and imposition of digitality, which oppose this in their own way, such a classical understanding of critique also seems to me to contradict the productive approach of media studies: It contradicts the approach of a subject that is concerned with the medial as the intermediary, so that not a core but an in-between matters, thus allowing processes of mediation to become the centre of attention. Critique in media studies must concern itself in every sense with processes of mediation.

For a critique of digitality that is attentive to these two forms of participation, it, therefore, becomes all the more important to address processes of reciprocity and interaction. The complexities and impositions of digitality challenge the very questions that acknowledge both my multifaceted participations *in* it and the limits of my perception and understanding *of* it. How will I know what I am involved in?

Critique of digitality is thus (at least) doubly involved in the unfolding of its concerns. It allows digitality to unfold by giving it space, inheriting its problems, and in the process reinforces—inevitably—the gesture of its urgency. Digital first, concerns second. Simultaneously, it is a matter of unfolding critique, and with it the complex of digitality, in such a way that all its compressions, densities, obfuscations and interweavings are allowed a different view.

For this process of unfolding, which is thus also a critique of current computerisation, the concepts of *interface* and *leiten* have a special and distinctive conceptual advantage, which I will develop in the following chapter: Thought together, they counter the pressing complexity of the present with their own multidimensionality and urgency of questioning.

Interface and *Leiten* 2

2.1 Interfaces (Levels of Connections)

What interfaces are can be seen in what they do. Interfaces create connections. They form and allow transitions and mediations. They also inevitably represent the separation of those very areas between which they allow passage.

Sounds familiar. The term interface has similarities with that of the medium, which media studies understands as that which intermediates. The medial is what is in between. In the act of mediating, what proves to be a medium is what can be absorbed into this process and may elude being perceived as a medium itself. Yet crucially there can be no neutral instance of mediation, as the medium in question will itself always shape the procedures and results of the mediation process.

However, positioning interface and medium even approximately on the same level as "the in-between, the interface, the intermedial, and ultimately as mediatisation" comes at a price (Hartmann 2014, p. 161). What is potentially lost by understanding an interface as merely a tool and gateway to the world—"as a sensor-motoric extension of our bodies and minds" (Jeong 2013, p. 220)—is the computer-related specificity of the term. This, however, is essential to its heuristic significance, especially when it comes to critiquing digitality.

Interfaces create interconnections thanks to which computers function and operate, are networked with other computers and are able to establish relationships with humans, other machines and other parts of the world beyond themselves. Interfaces perform mediation processes both to enable computer work and as part of it.

These connections can take the form of both software and hardware. Both are mutually dependent, because nothing would work without the processual materiality of the hardware executing the software, without which the hardware in turn could not compute. This is the basis of all currently possible interface configurations that have been summarised by Florian Cramer and Matthew Fuller (2008, p. 149) as interfaces between software and software, software and hardware, hardware and hardware, hardware and user, and software and user.

Software-software interfaces intermediate programmes, regulating the exchange of data between different applications. Especially application programming interfaces provide a good example: APIs, as part of software, define how data is transferred between individual programme modules. The protocol family TCP/IP (Transmission Control Protocol/Internet Protocol), according to whose rules computers connect and exchange data on the Internet, also belongs to this level of software-software interface that defines relationships between data handling processes.

Software-hardware interfaces determine how devices function and, as software, both govern and instruct the action of the hardware in question. Like a programmatic ghost in the machine and according to their laws, they allow devices to work and regulate, for example, the functioning of connected printers and scanners as "drivers".

Hardware-hardware interfaces, on the other hand, establish relationships between devices, for instance by allowing a USB interface to interconnect a computer and printer via a data cable, through which the software's signals are then conducted as electromagnetic waves, "codes [...] as sequences of signals" (Kittler 2008, p. 40).

Additional interface levels are required between hardware, software and user so that I can start to engage with a computer and pursue certain objectives with it. For this purpose, software and hardware create user interfaces—or, to be more precise and to highlight the techno-cultural aspects, they create forms of an "interface mise-en-scène" (Distelmeyer 2017, pp. 81–82) that address me visually and/or acoustically, so that I can perform inputs within a given framework and with given tools. Forms of signs offer themselves to me according to and (with)in the model of a certain form of interaction.

With their acoustic character strings, voice assistants offer a form of programmatic dialogue. Graphical user interfaces—the signs and symbols of the WIMP world (Windows, Icons, Menus, Pointers) found in conventional human-computer interaction (HCI)—appear as interface mises-en-scène on monitors in order to grant, instruct and regulate access and handling, for example in the form of the traditional desktop environment. Signs of what to do and how: As programmatic manifestations, which I understand along with Harun Farocki as "operational images" (cf. Distelmeyer 2017, pp. 92–98), the folders and files on the desktop or the app icons on the homescreen of a smartphone invite us to interact with them.

So by interacting with them (by talking, pressing, swiping, clicking, or gesturing), we interact with the computing devices. Interface mises-en-scène can thus be seen as performances that schedule and invite us to perform. Their processuality includes processes of the computer as well as the processes of human action both with and in them. This is made possible because we have at our disposal and command interfaces in the form of hardware that are adapted to people in a certain programmatic way through their functional shapes as for instance mouse, keyboard, touchscreen, microphone or camera. That this has symptomatic limits is shown, for example, by face recognition algorithms that had problems "recognising" People of Colour because of the selection used as their training data. Thus, our access to apparatuses can be implemented as a specific relationship, allowing us (not) to provide input.

At this level, the status of my actions is of no relevance and makes no difference. Whether I am allowed to occupy the ennobled and expert rank of programmer, or whether I am demoted to the humble position of clueless user, I always use and operate the interfaces that have been created. Just as the distinction between a graphical user interface and a programming language is "purely arbitrary" (Cramer and Fuller 2008, p. 150), the difference between users and programmers "is an effect of software" (Chun 2004, p. 38).

Cramer and Fuller (2008, p. 149), within the context of software studies, have coupled the five parts of their interface classification with an important reference to a problematic concept that to this day has unfortunately not been fully abandoned. In texts on media studies, this fifth form of interfaces, namely user interfaces, is often confused with the more elaborate and multifaceted *interface complex* and the notion of interface is thus simplified to no more than human-machine relations.

At this point it is necessary to add another reference; it refers to the growing presence of sensor-based technologies and practices, to the increasing proliferation of sensor-equipped computer formats that measure and convey the world through numerous hardware interfaces such as microphones, cameras and motion sensors. For what Cramer and Fuller classified as "hardware that connects users to hardware" (ibid.) extends today to everything that no longer has to make conscious use of this technology: Interfaces between hardware and "user" have long since become interfaces between hardware and the computable and mediated world.

Regardless of whether my movements are captured by the sensors in my smartphone, or the movements of the bees in the mentioned "hiveopolis", or the movements of humans/animals/objects recorded by the sensors in self-driving cars. The point is that input is no longer dependent on "users" in the traditional sense. It is not a question of conscious use and pursuit of purposes, but of purposeful setting (of the devices). Just what becomes input for these sensory computer formats, along with when and how, is decided by the hardware-software relationships that are created for precisely this purpose and primed for capture.

Thus the important distinctions of the highly generic term interface crucially expand into five forms of interfacing seen as five different process levels of connections. They operate not only

2.1 Interfaces (Levels of Connections)

within the various relationships of hardware and software for computers to function and to be networked, but also within the various relationships with the rest of the world into which functioning computers can enter, i.e. everything that is not a computer.

What these five interface levels have in common is that they are interconnected; combined, they form something with a unique complexity. A familiar problematic: It is this very complexity that shapes the first imposition of digitality, in the form of (over-)demanding multiplicity, presence and concealment of (pre-)conditions, apparatuses and processes that make digitality so difficult to grasp. Simply put, computers function through interfaces. Where computers operate, are networked with themselves and the outside world, interfaces operate.

Critique can gain something from this insight. Since this aspect of the complexity of digitality and computerisation operates thanks to the interface processes made possible by the five connection levels between hardware, software and the non-computer world, it is already possible, at this point, to outline a first differentiation. Addressing the complexity of interface processes is a way to relate to the complexity of digitality and computerisation.

What applies to the general concept of complexity—i.e. to address "the unity of a multiplicity of elements" that "refer to one another but cannot be reduced to one another" (Baecker 2018b, p. 2)—applies directly to the concept of the interface. It denotes the unity of a multiplicity and so demands that we pay attention to the processes at work at the various levels to be distinguished.

Another, no less important commonality of the levels on which the interface complex operates is their technical-material foundation, the indisputable basis which they share: The flow of electricity and the conduction of signals. From this follows a first, technical-material justification for thinking *interface* and *conduction* together—especially in the sense of the German word for "conducting", i.e. "leiten", which means in equal measure both the physical conduction of energy and the guiding related to leadership and control.

The functioning of electronic digital computers in all their forms is fundamentally dependent on the physical conduction of energy, and upon which each of the five interface levels is also dependent their own right: Current flows, electromagnetic waves propagate and are regulated, and signals/pulses are conducted through wires, cables, or wirelessly.

Thus, software-hardware interfaces steer and guide devices under the control of software. The fields between software and software—"before the point at which the protocol instructs decision-making, everything is equal" (Sprenger 2015, p. 23)—are mediated in this way. Hardware-to-hardware interfaces lay out connections for these signals/pulses. If something is to become input via hardware-to-world interfaces, it must be transformed into conductive pulses and signals for the attached computer. And in order for me as a user to be able to perceive those software manifestations created and laid out for me and my reaction on screens or via loudspeakers, they must be materialised through software and hardware interfaces.

Internally, and at the lowest level of computing, processes of *leiten* are also underway. Switching and guiding, the processors of all electronic digital computers consist of "a large set of switches" whose distinctive feature is "that they not only switch current, but *are also switched by current*" (Winkler 2015, p. 257). This routing of electrical impulses as signals allows programmes to operate. They set "the switches of the processor to the problem to be solved" and in this way momentarily *"turn the 'universal' into a special machine"* (ibid., p. 259). Consequently, Hartmut Winkler (ibid., p. 294) has called these conducting and guiding processes the "inner telegraphy" that rules inside the computer.

The programmability of those computers that today take on such diverse, quasi-autonomous forms, and that are both so widespread and deeply embedded, is thus in this sense also the automatability of switching and guiding electrical impulses. What computers do is essentially determined by how electricity is conducted.

This is precisely where the history of the term interface began. In the late 1860s, the physicists James and William Thomson (later Lord Kelvin) introduced the term "interface" to describe conditions of fluidity. Their focus was on surface conditions, conductivities and flow properties in an attempt to explain the conduction of energy, i.e. "interfaces between media of different conductivity" (Smith and Norton Wise 1989, p. 212).

For William Thomson, who adopted the term "interface as we may call it with Prof. James Thomson" from his older brother and first published it in a paper in 1874 (Thomson 1874, p. 442), the interface was both separating and connecting (cf. Hookway 2014, p. 85). As something which is in between and guiding, it thus performs a processing role, "turning molecules back or allowing them to pass through from either side" (Thomson 1874, p. 442). An important and far-reaching consequence of this investigation into connections for the transmission of energy was the development of telegraphy, which William Thomson drove forward as one of the directors of the Atlantic Telegraph Company. From the 1880s Thomson began to use the word interface to "refer to telegraph technology, yet his initial interest in the concept cannot be understood as independent from telegraphy" (Schaefer 2011, p. 165).

Questions and aspirations of *leiten* frame the beginning of the conceptual history of the interface. The five levels of the interface complex, all of which depend on and are oriented towards the conduction and flow capacity of states of electrical voltage, cannot be separated from this. However, this (ultimately fivefold) differentiation of the interface concept in the discourse on computer technology did not begin until a decade after the introduction of the ENIAC digital computer in 1946, and thus some 90 years after its first use by James and William Thomson.

"In computer technology", as Hans Dieter Hellige (2008, p. 13) points out, "*interface* first appeared in the course of the 1950s". The "initial physical emphasis" shaped "the term 'man-machine interface' that emerged shortly before 1960" (ibid.), which had also found its way into United States Air Force defence experiments in 1958—"to explore the problems and prospects for the 'man-machine interface'" (Mirowski 2002, p. 350).

Whereas the focus here was on relationships between humans and machines, in the course of the 1960s "the perspective of system and communication technology prevailed" (Hellige 2008, p. 13). Now the "man-computer interface" was thought of as a "boundary or transfer point between system and environment or between system components" and "its significance" was relativised in that it was "only one among many 'internal and external interfaces'"(ibid.), which was then specified, for example, as an "appropriate input-output interface" (Smith 1963, p. 344).

2.2 *Leiten* (Make Go)

The close connection between the terms interface and *leiten*, which as a German verb means equally "to conduct" and "to guide", therefore has both a conceptual-historical and a technical-material basis. The fact that computers operate by conducting electrical signals leads to the early conceptual history of the interface, which began to describe conductivity long before the introduction of electronic digital computers. From this, both terms (as an English-German pair of expressions) develop a special heuristic value in their coupling. It consists in raising not only historical and technical, but also power-analytical questions.

Thinking interface and *leiten* (and thus "to conduct" and "to guide") together points to a way of opening up the diverse processes of the historical and current presence of computer technologies. First and foremost, the notion of *leiten* suggests considering the materiality and processuality of the various interface levels of computer(isation), the infrastructures as well as processes, and thus also the flow and consumption of energy. *Leiten* can serve to remind us both of the conduits and circuits, of what is conducted through them, and for what purpose. In doing so, the term's two different levels of meaning prompt further questions that are vital to a critique of digitality and the ongoing processes of computerisation.

On the one hand, the verb *leiten* denotes physical processes: *Leiten* as conducting, as directing and channelling forces such as water and electrical voltage (cf. Schmidt 2015). In this way, and since Benjamin Franklin's early research on electricity around 1750, the English verb "to conduct" is translated into German as *leiten* (cf. Wilcke 1756). According to documents from the thirteenth century, the verb "has the meaning 'to conduct, to direct (a watercourse)'" (Ring 2009, p. 106). In the technical-physical

2.2 *Leiten* (Make Go)

sense, *leiten* is a form of channelled steering that promises control even when in flow.

The second level of meaning in *leiten* concerns the directing of other forces and movements, as in the guiding of living beings. The guiding of animals and people comes together in the image of the shepherd. The type of religious guidance referred to here also represents other political, ideological and pedagogical contexts. In this case, channelled steering becomes a form of social guidance. In his understanding of the term "conduct", Michel Foucault (1982, p. 789) refers in the same way to leading and guiding:

> Perhaps the equivocal nature of the term "conduct" is one of the best aids for coming to terms with the specificity of power relations. For to "conduct" is at the same time to "lead" others (according to mechanisms of coercion which are, to varying degrees, strict) and a way of behaving within a more or less open field of possibilities. The exercise of power consists in guiding the possibility of conduct and putting in order the possible outcome.

With this mode of conducting (as leading and guiding), the second literal sense of *leiten* as directing people (and oneself) is thus outlined. Similar to the technical-physical meaning of the word, the social meaning of *leiten* is also oriented towards how to direct what is going on. Thus, in line with the use of "governance" in the sixteenth century, *leiten* refers not only to political structures and to the administration of states, but also to the way "in which the conduct of individuals or of groups might be directed" (ibid., p. 790).

Keeping both levels of meaning in mind—the physical and the social—is especially helpful for a critique of digitality since every form of *leiten* as guiding that is made possible by means of computers is *only* possible thanks to the physical conduction of electrical voltage. At the same time, every human interaction with computers, in which inputs are made and signals are conducted, is part of a "power play" that I will describe in more detail as a movement between commanding and complying. The interlocking of flow and guide, of mediated signals and determining rules, which is essential for computers, and whose guiding qualities have long since affected far more than just human life, is expressed in the double meaning of *leiten*.

German linguistics of the nineteenth century traced the verb *leiten* back to "leittan" and "leitan", defining it "in its original meaning" or in the "proper sense" as "*to make go*" (Grimm and Grimm 1885). According to this understanding, *leiten* means "to make go, to set in motion, to lead, to escort, to accompany for be-ge-leiten" (Nikl 1866, p. 32). It can also be defined as an act of determining: "As an 'activum' or rather 'factitivum', to make go, i.e., to determine the direction of the movement of a goer, and in a broader sense, the direction of a movement in general, and indeed the whole movement itself." (Adelung 1808, p. 2023).

In this context, *leiten* encompasses definitions both "in relation to fluids, forces and the like, to which the imagination ascribes an independent movement, instructing them to follow a certain path with a certain goal", as well as "guiding" and "determining" as a social practice (Grimm and Grimm 1885). This is about power in many senses at once: It is about *making things go*, understood as directing and guiding through instructed and controlled movement.

The religious companion *Die Kunst des Leitens* focuses on this aspect. While *leiten* "means as much as 'to make go'", "the word 'führen' also stems from old High German, meaning 'to make go'", which is why both words refer accordingly to a movement "which the leader or guide is supposed to bring about" (Aigner 2011, p. 8). *Leiten* "therefore 'means to set people in motion'". (ibid., p. 9) Thus, by this logic, the processes that should ultimately matter are not those of leading or guiding at all. Rather, they are those that are to be made possible and caused by leading or guiding in the first place. *Making things go* has the future in its sights. *Leiten* is about "actions upon other actions "(Foucault 1982, p. 789).

The social level of meaning of *leiten*—in the sense of "leadership" as "determining a direction and a goal for a path" (Grimm and Grimm 1885)—can thus be described in other words as an ideological guidance. It serves the achievement of certain goals and purposes to which values are assigned. Ideological guidance is therefore, and in particular, clearly an exercise of power with a claim to leadership.

2.2 Leiten (Make Go)

However the extent to which this also applies to the physical sense of the word becomes clear in Herrmann Scheffler's *Die Naturgesetze und ihr Zusammenhang mit den abstrakten Wissenschaften*, dating from the second half of the nineteenth century. Here the conduction of electricity is described as a particular control of force. To distinguish conducting from radiating (*leiten* vs. *strahlen*), the mathematician and physicist Scheffler (1877, p. 386) explains the "conductivity of a body" ("Leitungsfähigkeit eines Körpers") as "the ability to form *standing waves* and consequently as the ability to hold its living force while propagating it."

Standing waves: Thus becomes true a contradiction that also applies to ideological guidance. The force is simultaneously transmitted *and* preserved. The power of *leiten*, of conducting and guiding, is to cause the spread of a force, the maintenance of which can be controlled at the same time. *To make go* is both at the same time: To set in motion and to hold.

In this way, different modes of control come into effect. Techniques of the Self, confession or introspection and self-guidance through the internalisation of values, rules and laws spring to mind. Other techniques, on the other hand, are used to ensure the success of physical *leiten*. Here, the same material can be used to conduct as well as measure.

Cables, which "criss-cross, are networked and which are multi-branched" wherever "electricity is to be conducted, whether as energy or as a signal," are the best example of this (Gethmann and Sprenger 2014, p. 7). For cables, with a double function that is "crucial in the history of science, serve not only to transmit, but also and always to measure the process of transmission." (ibid., pp. 29–30). It was discovered around 1820 that a compass needle reacts to the current in a cable, and from that point on a "magnetic needle could be used as an indicator of the current" (Bexte 2002, p. 30). By thus combining electricity with magnetism, the galvanometer made "internal states of cables visible and thus 'acquirable as a system of information'"(ibid., p. 31).

For a critique of digitality, this provides a new angle of approach for addressing the complexity of the challenge. The close connection between the terms interface and *leiten* demands attention be paid to interconnected processes. This connection calls to mind the different, sometimes inaccessible levels and materialities of the interface complex. It asks about the ways and procedures of conducting and guiding and also about what or who is being conducted/guided here. And since this question is aimed at software and hardware connections as well as at life forms in their encounters with these connections, it offers the advantage of a particular, power-analytical focus.

This is because the conceptual coupling of interface and *leiten* raises questions of power even where they would otherwise not necessarily arise. However, power is not to be confused with domination. Instead, the concept of power here denotes a "more-or-less coordinated [...] cluster of relations" (Foucault 1980, p. 199) intended to secure influence and confirm leadership. Again, as with interfaces, it depends on processes and conditions; the exercise of power is a "structure of actions brought to bear upon possible actions" (Foucault 1982, p. 789).

Because *leiten* is a form of power in this sense, questions of power naturally also arise when the discussion is supposedly only about technology, about tools or about usability as "fitness for use" (Robben and Schelhowe 2012, p. 12). Such ongoing attention to power relations is highly appropriate for any critical engagement with computers. And in order to gauge the strategic consequences for a critique of digitality that arise from approaching the interface complex through questions of *leiten*, it is therefore necessary to at least briefly outline the connections between digitality and power.

2.3 Power (Commanding and Complying)

Computers are associated with aspirations of power in a variety of ways. The hopes for the collection, evaluation and (instantaneous) consequences of huge amounts of data, the reduction and control of (human) work processes through the diverse forms of computer-

2.3 Power (Commanding and Complying)

based automation and networking are enduring examples. The developments of algorithmic governmentality and capture capitalism, cybernetic control technologies as a governing machine, the homophily of Big Data, and the future solidification of a patterned past through the training procedures of machine learning, which have already been outlined and critiqued, testify to claims to power.

The same applies to the pressure of urgency through which digitalisation is promoted firstly as being without alternative, and secondly through either the computer or the Internet as the "leading medium" (Müller and Ligensa 2009, p. 11). However this urgency is also only a further, (re)current consequence of fundamental demands and uses of power that characterise computer technology. Its decisive programmability allows the most diverse applications to be handled by the same kind of machine, and precisely in this way—with the multiplicity of functions of the general purpose machine—affirms its supremacy over other technical forms. This marks the first fundamental connection between computer technology and questions of power.

However, the supposedly unrestricted scope of the "universal machine" is already problematic (cf. Winkler 2004a, p. 207). The expectation that computers can be used for any purpose is a significant shift in the claim to universality founded on the programmability of a computing machine. In his time, Alan Turing (1950, p. 439) had mathematically explained the "universality of digital computers" in 1950 by stating that "these machines can do all sorts of things that a human computer could do" (ibid., p. 436). Universality within the framework of the computable has since developed into the universality of computability.

The alleged omnipotence of the computer, through which the boundaries of the calculable seem to dissolve, is not, however, a relatively recent phenomenon of electronic digital computers. It began even before they were created. For in the mid-nineteenth century, Ada Lovelace had not only written the first programme in computer (pre)history by publishing a table for calculating Bernoulli numbers for Charles Babbage's plans for his "Analytical Engine". Moreover, in this context, Lovelace had already speculated in 1843 on the possibilities of programming this calculating machine to be a composer. One machine for everything. She suggested that "the engine might compose elaborate and scientific pieces of music of any degree of complexity or extent" (Lovelace 1842).

Secondly, computer technology is fundamentally linked to claims to power because of the nature of its programmability. Orders are obeyed. Wendy Chun (2013, pp. 29–34) has drawn attention to the history of the "Yes, Sir" logic at work here, tracing it back to the programmers and operators of the first electronic digital computer, ENIAC, in the mid-1940s. Under the direction of a chief programmer Kathleen McNulty, Frances Bilas, Betty Jean Jennings, Elizabeth Snyder, Ruth Lichterman, and Marlyn Wescoff were responsible for determining the switching and conducting procedures of the ENIAC, still performed manually (see Fig. 2.1).

Conducting, switching, and obeying: Beginning in 1947, before programmes could be coded by merely "flipping a switch, which corresponded to sixty stored instructions" (Chun 2004, p. 28), these first female programmers, the so-called "ENIAC girls," took care of the planning and execution of the replugging

Fig. 2.1 Ruth Lichterman and Marlyn Wescoff (standing) in 1946 programming the ENIAC by reconnecting cables. (Photo: ARL Technical Library)

2.3 Power (Commanding and Complying)

of cables necessary for the ENIAC to perform these instructions. The command structure as well as the desire for uncontradicted operation thus entered the organisational structure of modern computers. As switching and conducting became automated and computers could receive, store, and execute commands by the same means, "Yes, Sir" became virtually the metaprogramme of programmability:

> One could say that programming became programming and software became software when commands shifted from commanding a "girl" to commanding a machine. The image above reveals the dream of "programming proper"—a man sitting at a desk giving commands to a female "operator". Software languages are based on a series of imperatives that stem from World War II command and control structure. (ibid., p. 33).

The third fundamental connection between computer technology and questions of power follows on from this, becoming apparent in the way human interaction with these programmable machines is organised.

This encounter with computer technology—celebrated in the 1990s and 2000s with the buzzwords "interaction" and "interactivity" (cf. Distelmeyer 2012, pp. 139–189)—is based on the striking interplay of those two interface levels that mediate between hardware and user, and between software and user (cf. Cramer and Fuller 2008). People gain access to and negotiate with software processes through hardware such as the touchscreen, monitor, camera, mouse, trackpad, keyboard, speaker, or microphone.

This is how my interaction with the programmability of this computer is brought into being, as it cannot operate without the other interface levels between software and hardware. Moreover, the fact that the functioning of software on my computer is increasingly dependent on my device being connected to others via the internet, because software increasingly operates as a cloud service, further deepens and reinforces the interlocking of the interface levels, as I will show in the third chapter.

No matter, however, whether the software I interact with by means of hardware runs on my computer or on a server networked with it, the space of potentialities offered by user interfaces always realises a *logic and aesthetics of command* through which dealing with computers becomes in principle a power play (cf. Distelmeyer 2017, pp. 65–126 and Distelmeyer 2018).

Every human-computer interaction is predisposed by the rules of programming and defined hardware-software relationships. That and how I am able to react to what is made available to me by means of user interfaces, that and how computers and their features manifest themselves to me, has thus been provided for by programming. My freedom of action exists only because and insofar as it is granted. It cannot be otherwise, because the adjustable machine must also have been adjusted for just that—for my purpose—beforehand.

Everywhere where I want to be active in and with interfaces or am captured by them without any intervention on my part, programming has determined both the ways and means. Not only the performance of any programme, but also the means of launching it, for example, by tapping the touchscreen of my smartphone, are based on the same, clearly defined logic. Thus, computers are always already bound to "rules, regulations for execution, algorithms" and, in order for humans to participate, they can "liberate the rule from its latency and bring it to the surface of readable program texts" (Winkler 2004, p. 152).

This aspect of the rule-like is of great importance for the connection between physical and ideological modes of *leiten*, to which I will return later. For if and as long as computers depend on humans who (with "user" status) make conscious inputs via interfaces designed for them, computers must thereby somehow convey rules and ideas about how the relationship between humans and computers is intended and should be managed here. They guide people in their interaction with such technology.

The computer scientist and computer (art) activist Frieder Nake (2021/1984, p. 283) has repeatedly asserted this since the 1980s: What and how a human enters into the computer, the computer will use "under the direction of the program" for entries (understood as "assignments of values to parameters") and decisions (understood as "ramifications in the program"). How data then "acquire this meaning within the computer has been deter-

2.3 Power (Commanding and Complying)

mined by the programmer in this way and not otherwise" (ibid.). This is why Nake has described in 1984 as a "helpless formula for a profoundly social process" (ibid., p. 286), the "human-machine communication" that preceded the interaction hype of the 1990s: "The parties who connect through communicative interfaces are not so much the computer and its operator as the operator and the programmer" (ibid., p. 284).

This idea of a human individual, "the programmer", who possesses a dominant overview and insight has, of course, been under pressure for a long time. Overviews and insights dwindle—as well as the procedures differentiate themselves—into cooperative programming and into automated processes.

The hope of algorithmic decision-making attached to AI, artificial neural networks and machine learning processes, that "in the future, computers will have to be programmed less and less in order to fulfil certain tasks or solve problems, but will instead operate quasi-autonomously with self-learning algorithms" (Sudmann 2018b, p. 55), is geared towards achieving machine autonomy. New claims to power herald the prospect of self-programming computers, thus also provoking fears of the recursive self-improvement of a "superintelligent AI" (Tegmark 2017, p. 438). In 2018, the AI application "Bayou" was unveiled, which is capable by way of machine learning of programming itself, of writing its own programme lines (cf. Murali et al. 2018).

Nevertheless, this does not change the fact that even such momentous possibilities must first be wanted, provided for, infrastructurally created, maintained and supplied with power by humans. Humans remain responsible, and it is worth bearing in mind that "Bayou", for example, was developed at Rice University in Houston with the financial support of Google and the Defence Advanced Research Projects Agency (DARPA) of the US Department of Defence.

At the same time, these developments underpin the fundamental importance of *decisive programmability,* in that they both exploit and emphasise the determinability of indeterminate machines, thanks to which software, hardware and their usage are—flexibly, yet bindingly related to each other. Programmability is the computer's power as a multifunctional machine. This is precisely why there is a certain chutzpah in even calling the methods of dealing with computers thus made possible "interaction".

It doesn't matter whether I'm writing with a word processor, communicating via social media platforms, using my navigation device, moving around in an Open World computer game, gesticulating in front of my Kinect camera or programming in a high-level programming language: Interaction here is not so much acting in relation to something else, but rather acting with intention for something else. In order for the computer, firstly, to recognise and process my actions as actions at all and, secondly, to be able to communicate its activities to me via interface systems, previsions have been made for this already in the programming. The ADM development of pattern recognition, thanks to which voice control works, is no exception. Even programmatic autonomy, this form of quasi-independent advancement, must have been granted beforehand by programming—as taking action upon other actions.

Everything runs according to the rules, even the freedom I have to choose what I want to do:

> Since Alan Turing's sensational construction of a discrete machine and John von Neumann's implementation of a decision-safe functional logic, the Turing machine model has represented a universal computing machine that decomposes intelligence into elementary, performable arithmetic operations. The symbolic space that emerges inside it is a purely numerical one. Here everything is strictly determined, pre-calculated and calculated […]. The set of possible interactions is completely defined by mathematically determined rules. (Maresch 2004, p. 280).

Interaction with the computer thus means allowing oneself to become involved in conditions of possibility that are programmatically determined. That is why the commanding of what computers offer is always linked to acts of compliance. Thanks to programmability, however, this compliance is by no means to be understood as a one-way street. Rather, there are detours, side paths, and ways out through which conditions and therefore power play can change.

2.3 Power (Commanding and Complying)

Fig. 2.2 Facebook without interaction metrics: Screenshot from Benjamin Grosser's video documentary "Facebook Demetricator" (Grosser 2018)

Benjamin Grosser's "Facebook Demetricator", a now canonical piece of software art developed in 2012, is a convincing example of this. As a programmed add-on, a software extension for browsers, the "Demetricator" changes Facebook's appearance (cf. Figure 2.2).

At the push of a button, a Facebook page shows up entirely without the infamous statistics, without the ubiquitous totals of "posts," "likes," and "friends" that otherwise characterise this mode of being social, and its metric logic of function. Furthermore it is precisely by being able to be turned on and off that statistics can be interrogated as to their relevance to Facebook's mode of social interaction. The experience of "how the absence of metrics change our interactions within networked space" is at the same time the experience that programming is modifiable (Grosser 2014).

Thus, programmability shows itself as regulating of change that is, in principle, always possible. In order to understand "micro-decisions" as the smallest unit and technical prerequisite of the "politics of networks", Florian Sprenger (2015, p. 71) quotes the computer scientist Agata Królikowski with her reference to programmatic variability: The difference between "blocking information, delaying information and conducting information is merely a technical rule definition in software that can be changed at any time".

Precisely because in the context of digitality all forms of rule-making run on the basis of programmability, they can also be circumvented or changed on this very same basis. The formation of the non-explicitly stipulated inherent dynamics of Machine Learning also draws on this, and any form of hacking, of modifying intervention into computer systems, enables this worry or hope to come true. *Yes, Sir!* As a receiver of commands, computers take their orders without objection, including from hackers, of course. Thus, computers allow for a potentially endless shifting between command and compliance; a power play in which I give the machine orders, follow its rules, and can change them (with new orders) because I am in principle (and also for this) part of the plan.

How we as humans, vis-à-vis this sort of machine, can be and become effective thus necessitates the creation of a twofold model. These machines have to be shaped according to our claims to power, and an equally effective model of us as a graspable and thus influential counterpart is anchored within them. (cf. Nake 2021/1984, p. 115; Budde and Züllighoven 1990, p. 4; Pias 2000, p. 104).

2.4 Depresenting (Conceal and Disclose)

Something of both the modelling of the machine and its human correlate must make itself felt in this power play. If the somewhat euphemistically termed interaction is to work, the planned relationship between humans and computers must be on display in some way. What software is supposed to be able to do needs to be conveyed.

This is due to the Janus-faced nature of the computer, which causes a sort of mediation emergency. The human use of the computer is dependent on transfer processes between two levels. Frieder Nake (2021/2016, p. 125) has distinguished them as *surface* and *subface*: "The surface is analog, the subface is digital".

2.4 Depresenting (Conceal and Disclose)

Therefore, "computer things" exist "dually" in that "they have a side that is sensually accessible to us and a side that is sensually inaccessible to us" (Nake 2021/2001, p. 24).

To analytically distinguish between memory content (electrical impulses that can be processed as "data") and aesthetic phenomena (as surface effects of human-computer interfaces) is at the same time to acknowledge their "ontological togetherness" (Nake 2021/2016, p. 138). This "new coupling system", according to Yuk Hui (2015, pp. 15–16), calls for "a new questioning of aesthetics that must also take account of its technical condition".

As long as computers (need to) require humans to make inputs, they also need to provide people with information about how such inputs can be made. They reveal something of their systematics, so that outsiders can play along and exert influence according to the rules of the systematics. I am thus informed by computers to some extent about what I should engage with so that my engagement can in turn have an effect. The designs of user interfaces, the interface mises-en-scène of spaces of possibility, plays a decisive role in this.

Friedrich Kittler has criticised these interfaces that have dominated up to now for paradoxically distancing people from computers. For Kittler, the graphical user interfaces that have prevailed since the early 1980s, these particularly obtrusive manifestations of software as graphical spaces for action, systematically remove and restrict what is essential to the computer. This essence is its (in Turing's sense universal) programmability, a kind of mathematical freedom. The "indispensability and, consequently, the priority of hardware" (Kittler 1993, p. 237) is hidden by the software (of high-level programming languages). In the form of operating systems, software also ensures that the basically open—albeit restricted—machine becomes a *closed shop* in which only certain uses are possible.

From Kittler's perspective, the smokescreens of user interface thus conceal two things: Access to the programmability of the essentially egalitarian machine called the computer, and secondly the desire for power by software corporations to turn humans as "users" into subjects of their operating systems. According to Kittler (1986, pp. 7–8), in that "surface effect, as it is received by consumers under the beautiful name of interface", in that "dazzle" of pictorial user interfaces, hidden commands have ensured that commands from outside are prevented:

> You can not even enter any command at that point. The commands are already pre-selected by the images, the icons. The average person doesn't even notice that. But that doesn't mean that a thousand other things aren't possible on the Mac, as soon as you go down to the symbolic level of verbal textual programming. The user interface, however, creates the impression that this level beneath the images does not exist at all. (Kittler 1994b, p. 120).

Kittler's (1994a, p. 210) criticism, that through the graphical user interface and by using "keywords such as user interface, user friendliness or even data protection" industry has meanwhile "condemned humans to remain humans," touches on an important point. It attacks the relationship between software and ideology where the lack of mediation is supposed to be solved by interface mises-en-scène. The models for this do not originate from computer relationships, to which Kittler still refers when discussing the command line, but are obtrusively anthropocentric.

Without doubt, the influence of these operational images is immense, which can now—as a consequence of the relations between the terms interface and *leiten*—be understood as operational and conducting and guiding images. However, the "surface effect" criticised by Kittler does not simply construct any form of "to remain human".

In contrast, by dealing with the desktop and such operational images in the form of files, folders, and trash, we have been and continue to be "condemned" to that very particular form of becoming human beings: Office workers. Computer work is office work in that the "graphically intuitive MacIntosh interface" constructs a reality "by and for white middle- and upper-class users to replicate a world that they know and feel comfortable within" (Selfe and Selfe 1994, p. 486). This is what empowerment looks like. Fittingly, a promo video for the new computer called Lisa, which Apple first used to introduce the desktop mise-en-scène and the mouse in 1983, had a senior, *white* manager spent 15 min explaining the innovations (see Fig. 2.3). What was so special

2.4 Depresenting (Conceal and Disclose)

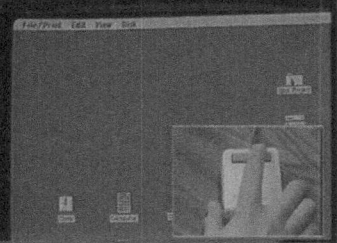

Fig. 2.3 'Works the way I do': Screenshots from the promo video for the Apple Lisa (Apple Computer Inc. 1983).

about this new system? "You see, it works the way I do." (cf. Apple Computer Inc. 1983).

Interfaces and operating systems do "produce 'users'—one and all" (Chun 2013, pp. 67–68). This ideological structure by which a user interface "is not only defined by but also actively defines what is human and what is machine" (Hookway 2014, p. 12) specifically mediates between two forms of *leiten*. On the one hand, the interface mise-en-scène guides me on how to interact with the computer. On the other hand, the clickable files on the desktop and the touchable app icons on the homescreen of my smartphone can only do this because they are indexical (cf. Peirce 1998, p. 5): They are causally and physically connected to my smartphone's internal conduction processes. They are in contact with the internal telegraphy of the computer.

In other words, the specific operativity of those operational and indexical (conducting and guiding) images that interface mises-en-scène create and offer brings together two different forms of operations: The operations in and between computers on the one hand, and human action on the other. Although human action must in principle be distinguished from the programme-controlled action of computers, in this case it can also be understood as a (guided) operation because it occurs in relation to this technology, which "conflates *programmability* and *formalisability*" (Mersch 2016, p. 35).

The disappointed conclusion that dealing with graphical user interfaces condemns humans to remain mere humans therefore does not go far enough. The pictorial context into which these interface formations acclimate is rather the programmatic pictorial context of a somewhat more complicated (wishful) constellation: Of humans interacting with computers, and of computers allowing human access. This is why interface mises-en-scène offer both ideological access and access to ideological critique.

Interface mises-en-scène realise operational models of the relationship between people and computers. They convey software as what people can do with it. They pursue the intention of making this relationship work, and therefore cannot help but exhibit something of this intention. "[T]he [black] box begs to be touched, it exists to be manipulated, to be *interfaced*." (Galloway 2011, p. 239) The way in which humans, computers and their relationship to each other are conceived here is shown in the mises-en-scène that are supposed to make this relationship true, meaning, in this context, effective.

The reason for this lies in the operativity and indexicality of these images. They are not only meant for looking at (and understanding), but for processes of humans and machines operating with them. They fulfill themselves in these roles, and are therefore dependent on a certain understanding and resulting action.

Because their aesthetic appearance as both image and sign (e.g. in the form of the operational image of a camera on the touch screen of my smartphone) is causally as well as physically connected to the internal switching and conduction processes of the computer (and I can thus launch the programme and make photographic use of my smartphone's camera sensors) the programmed relationship between human and machine, which is understood in some way by me as a "user," can be fulfilled in this way. On the basis of such programmatic indexicality, the images of the interface mises-en-scène are "operative images that are absorbed in the technical execution, that are needed for an operation" (Farocki 2004, p. 61).

That this would make neither represent the systematics of the computer at work here, nor those of the software, or even—to use another mythical buzzword—make it "transparent" is perfectly clear. However in precisely these moments of (inter)action, which Kittler (1994b, p. 120), as a fan of the command line, calls the

2.4 Depresenting (Conceal and Disclose)

deprivation of the machine by "the images", something is also offered to us. We encounter programming and design-turned-ideas of how the human relationship to computers and their programmes should look, be understood, and become tangible.

What happens in the formation of user interfaces is therefore not only a deception. Here, concealment and disclosure occur at the same time. User interfaces, as introduced by Marianne van den Boomen (2014, p. 36), *depresent*. At the same moment that interfaces with their operational (conducting and guiding) images invite me to set machine processes in motion for a specific and intended purpose (e.g. to take photographs), they conceal these processes (of internal telegraphy) and, according to van den Boomen, present ontologised entities in order to function as human-readable signs:

> In the case of computer icons such a disclosure of the hidden processes would kill the principle of the shortcut, making it illegible by the obfuscating stream of messages about ongoing (or halted) machine processes. The concealment of processes is not contingent, it is a purposive construction to withhold particular representations, built in by interfacial design. I propose to call this built-in principle depresentation, in order to distinguish it from contingent non-representation. (ibid.)

Kittler's important observation that corporations like Microsoft—whose operating systems and programmes/apps strive to make us their "subjects"—face the problem of "how to conceal from the subjects the subjugation that will enable them to triumph worldwide" (Kittler 1994a, p. 211) is only one half of the problem. The other half consists in presenting oneself to "the subjects" in such a way that the latter participates (and in certain ways). Only thus, through participation, are the intended and promised exertions of power fulfilled.

The aesthetic appearance of software, of operating systems and programmes/apps, addresses me so that I—be it as a "subject", beneficiary or servant of Microsoft, Apple, Alphabet, Huawei, Alibaba among others—engage in what I accept as natural and functional processes in order to exert my influence and issue my orders myself. *I just work.*

The dual function that William Thomson defined as the function of the interface at the end of the nineteenth century, turning back and allowing to pass, takes on a new dimension here. In the case of graphical user interfaces, the simultaneous separating and mediating effect is realised aesthetically as depresentation. In a depresenting way, claims to power are both fulfilled and deprived, and interface mises-en-scène oscillate between concealing and disclosing. In this way, they enable the power play of commanding and complying by combining physical conducting with ideological guidance, i.e. through modes of *leiten*.

The term play is meant to emphasise the negotiation process in which power relations here become real. Pre-regulations and conditions, programmes and modes of operation are all realised through the interaction with human-computer interfaces, which then both produces the opposites "human" and "computer" envisaged therein, and is then able also to search for ways out, to find gaps in the system and to evade its stipulations. What, according to Roland Barthes (1977, p. 162), is true for every text—it has some sort of clearance, "like a door, like, a machine with 'play'"—is true for human-computer interfaces in a specific, programmatic way.

As long as interface mises-en-scène address people, because we are called upon to provide input, they make the relationship to be established both present and negotiable in a certain, limited and intentional way. Here, in this invitation to participate, there is therefore inevitably also an opportunity to intervene and to interrogate. User interfaces in particular can thus be used as an invitation to investigate the planned relationship between humans and computer(isation), in which user interfaces are just as much a part as all other levels of interfacing. They open a path to the critique of digitality.

2.5 Interfacing (Conducting and Guiding)

The understanding that interfaces perform modes of *leiten*, conducting and guiding, has productive consequences for a critique of digitality. They follow from the range of meanings of this

2.5 Interfacing (Conducting and Guiding)

English-German pair of expressions and their relations to each other. This connection between interface and *leiten* affirms and pointedly reinforces an insight that has since become accepted in media studies: An interface is not a thing or a condition, but always a process that runs, thanks to things and conditions, and that has effects. (cf. Galloway 2012; Drucker 2014; Emerson 2014; Ash 2015; Wirth 2016b; Distelmeyer 2017; Ernst and Schröter 2017; Kaerlein 2018). The processuality of interfaces, the *interfacing*, which enable the workings of computers on the interconnected levels between hardware, software, and the non-computer world, takes place in modes of conducting and guiding.

Interfaces perform modes of *leiten* by making processors work, creating internal connections, transmitting rules, pairing apparatuses, opening accesses as well as instructing what to do and how to do it. To break it down more precisely, four *fields of leiten* have emerged from the five *levels of interfaces* already identified. Unlocking them and thus describing the different levels of the interface complex with the twofold meaning of physical conduction and ideological guidance opens up a new point of access to the presence of computer(isation) and its critique.

I separate the four fields of *leiten* here in order to distinguish theoretically what overlaps practically in the workings of computers. This distinction becomes all the more important as the process of computerisation advances. For one vanishing point of this development is precisely that the interdependent fields tend to overlap beyond recognition.

The first field includes all processes of conduction concerning internal telegraphy. This is the field of transmissions of those impulses and signals inside (the various forms) of the computer for which interfaces are created between hardware and hardware, hardware and software, and software and software. In this field, software can determine the functioning of devices, and operating systems define conditions and limits of operations.

The second field of *leiten* is the logical extension of the first: The resulting interconnection and conduction processes between computers and within the networks connecting them. Cables and wireless connections—via air interfaces—ensure the propagation of the electromagnetic waves that carry the internet. Fibre optic cables connect to transmission towers so that the 5G project can succeed as a "blanket covering of the electromagnetic field with waves that are increasingly information-rich." (Schneider 2020, p. 357). They transmit what happens inside computers, where in turn it is received back, and for which purpose, as a protocol-based data transfer via micro-decisions, must satisfy the conditions of TCP/IP.

In a way, this was bound to happen. Because the computer with its internal telegraphy "fuses the space of telecommunication with the inner workings of the machine itself", its "wiring" is for Hartmut Winkler (2015, pp. 293–294) not an add-on but a consequence that is inherent from the beginning. Here, interface configurations between hardware and software become externalised, for which new interface constellations such as underwater cables, air interfaces and internet protocols, for example, have emerged.

However, when computers are programmed by computers and thus guided to new procedures and purposes with hardware and software interfaces, such processes of *leiten* between computers expand dramatically. Because in this way, physical conduction between computers definitively coincides with ideological guidance that establishes assumptions, procedures, and goals. Insofar as this can be done by circumventing human activity and responsibility—which in one way or another has so far been characteristic of ideological guidance—this gives the field of *leiten* between computers as external telegraphy a new, immensely significant dimension in terms of power relations. It also and especially concerns the third field of *leiten*.

In this third field, the conduction processes take place between (networked) computers and everything that is not a computer. In addition to the interface levels that ensure the programmatic functioning of internal and external telegraphy, the interfaces between hardware and the mediatable and investigable world are especially important here. Things and bodies connected to (networked) computers are controlled and in turn provide input. Examples range from "smart" homes, pacemakers and hearing aids, to brain-computer interfaces. Jennifer Gabrys calls this proliferation of the relationship between the mediatable and investigable world and the sensor-based computer technology "environmentalization".

2.5 Interfacing (Conducting and Guiding)

She speaks of "the *becoming environmental of computation*" (Gabrys 2016, p. 4).

Cybernetic control loops close and open up themselves to further implications. Networked and sensor-equipped street lamps of a smart city record movements in their surroundings, provide light when needed and forward their survey results, their "knowledge" of the city (cf. Bauer 2017). Methods of "virtual fencing" record and guide farm animals within the boundaries of a virtual fence, which now no longer needs to be physically erected because it can be set up flexibly and monitored individually for both herds and single animals (cf. Friedrich 2021). Machine learning is the way in which such relational boundaries are being extended, ultimately dissolving into a single, expansive relationship.

This field of *leiten* is growing immensely—it's supposed to be the world: "It's Everywhere. It's Invisible. It's Ubicomp." (Weiser 1997). The intended ubiquity of computers as a new ecology both permeated and determined by technology is based on this premise. Under the headings *technosphere* and *technoecology*, this proliferation, embedding, and momentum of computer technology is understood as "implication" (Hansen 2015, pp. 580–629), and a third phase of the cybernetic "culture of control" (Hörl 2016, p. 41). Thus, for techno-ecological approaches to media studies, "media become an environment that we experience simply by being and acting in space and time" (Hansen 2013, p. 73).

Phrases such as environmentalisation, technoecology, and technosphere indicate that this third field includes all processes of *leiten* which occur and mediate between computers and non-computers. Strictly speaking then, this would include all relations between humans and computers. However, it is useful and important for at least two reasons to examine this part of the third field with particular attention, and to highlight it as a fourth field of *leiten*.

A critique of digitality that understands itself as an involved unfolding of its concern must be especially interested in the realm in which the encounter between humans and computers takes place. This encounter is the very basis of such critique, not merely its object or subject. In addition, it is in this fourth field that processes of physical conducting explicitly combine with those of ideological guiding. It is here that particular forms and consequences of programmability occur. To emphasise human-machine relations separately as a fourth field of *leiten*, and thus also to emphasise the responsibility of programming, therefore helps precisely to describe the changes implied by a shift from programming to self-programming.

This fourth field of *leiten* therefore includes in particular the processes of conscious negotiation between humans and computers. Both in contrast and addition to those phenomena in which people become part of the act of capturing—via sensory interfaces between hardware and the mediatable, investigable world—without providing conscious input via user interfaces, it is a matter here of processes that are not only technically prearranged.

Here an aesthetic dimension is added, which is programmed and designed according to certain ideas of value and purpose. My interaction with computers is made possible by hardware/software configurations, which also include such software manifestations that allow me voice control, or that open up a sphere of interaction in which I can exert gestural influence in front of a camera or by means of mouse, keyboard and touchscreen. *It works the way I do.* In this area of user interfaces and interface mises-en-scène, operational images unfold their guiding effect.

The necessary indexicality of these images interlocks technical-physical conducting and ideological guiding. Commanding and complying: The operational images—be it on a desktop interface, in the design of a website, in the space of action of a computer game, or on the homescreen of a smartphone—always transmit concepts. By mediating human-computer relations, they place humans and machines into designated positions, acting out models and integrating world views into this particular form of "useful images" (cf. Nohr 2014).

The fact that *leiten* also has an ideological dimension here can be easily observed in interface mises-en-scène such as the desktop, the tile and grid aesthetics of apps or other such appearances. Notions of, for example, work (at a desk) and interaction (as command-and-comply) are brought to the fore, which at the same time should be overlooked in favour of usability. As if it were a

2.5 Interfacing (Conducting and Guiding)

tool and not an implemented concept. Mark Weiser's (1994) symptomatic credo of "invisible interfaces" suggests, not least, that operational images should please disappear in the process of their purpose and should by no means attract attention as images. The third chapter will explore this in more detail using the example of the introduction of the iPhone and its app grid.

Another form of ideological guidance, the communication of ideals and regulations, is involved in those moments when programming occurs. For by programming, I instruct computers with user interfaces designed for this purpose to proceed in this way and not in any other way. I determine sequences, establish relationships, define if-then conditions, assign values, and thus pursue a specific goal for which I temporarily specify the general purpose machine. I try to implement purposes by enacting rules. I make computers go.

Thus, because programme scripts conflate "legislation with execution" (Chun 2013, p. 128), a responsibility emerges that justifies distinguishing this fourth field of *leiten* from the third. When people programme, they combine ideological guiding with physical conducting. They transform ideas of purpose, goal, and value into switching and conducting processes for automated operations. In this way, computer processes are determined such that as a consequence they (should) take place in the different fields of *leiten* and become usable, for example, in the form of programmed user interfaces as a relationship between ideological guidance and physical conduction.

All this can only succeed with the participation of defined and determinative interfaces, which (especially in higher programming languages) make programming possible at all. Human and human-made technology thus stand jointly responsible for programming, that particular execution of power being a programmatic action upon other actions.

Within this framework, humans remain responsible even if they programme and train an artificial neural network whose internal conduction processes and computational steps then run "autonomously" and can elude human comprehension. The steps towards autonomisation that are currently being developed in AI or ADM research are not outside such responsibility. However, software that is designed for recursive self-improvement, and whose programme could thus allow a desired configuration of "autonomous" self-programming would represent an entirely new step.

With that step, when this ideological guidance of programming takes place entirely through the machines themselves, i.e. "computers as source of source code" (ibid., p. 38), the vision of the technosphere as an environmental and total culture of control becomes complete. It is all a question of relation: As far as the processes of programming are concerned, there is then no longer any difference between the second and the fourth field of *leiten*. Physical conduction and ideological guidance become one.

This obviously has far-reaching consequences for the possibilities of a society to debate and dispute the exercise of power. The momentum of programmatic processes, which is currently being advanced with the use of machine learning techniques, ultimately means placing this form of power outside any arena for discussion. The problems already being negotiated in particular at European Union level (cf. EK 2018a, b), such as being able to behave in relation to algorithms that IT companies guard as their trade secrets and which can no longer be traced in detail in artificial neural networks, are thus reaching a new dimension (cf. Engemann 2018, p. 254). Discourse becomes supplanted in this way by device-based processes of conducting and switching.

2.6 Question Mode (Interface Analyses)

After this necessary detour via the connections between digitality and power, depresentation and fields of *leiten*, it should hopefully now be clearer to what extent the close, historical and conceptual connection between the terms interface and *leiten* paves the way for a critique of digitality. The present state of computer(isation) can be described as processes of *leiten* that take place in four fields and are dependent on five interface levels.

Where computers operate, interfaces also operate and run procedures of *leiten*. Without them, no computer can process, no software can inhabit the hardware. Without them, nothing and no one

2.6 Question Mode (Interface Analyses)

can give instructions or input to this kind of machine, be it as an act of programming, as sensing processes, or as input by means of those use-everyday interfaces that address, construct and programmatically empower users. Without them, there is no connection whatsoever, neither to local networks or the internet, nor to connections with things or living beings. Without them, neural networks can neither be set up (i.e. programming computers to do so), nor trained, nor run. Without them, none of what computerisation promises as a technosphere runs.

The functions of what has been called "post-interface" in recent discussions is also a co-dependent in this relationship. Those "media that no longer presuppose the active *user* operating via the interface, but expect a body that can become an output of medial operations precisely through its passivity and in the mode of this passivity" (Andreas et al. 2018, pp. 8–9) still remain dependent on the connection between interfaces and processes of *leiten*. For this reason Christian Ulrik Andersen and Søren Pold (2018, p. 10) speak of the "metainterface":

> Although the interface may seem to evade perception, and become global (everywhere) and generalized (in everything), it still holds a textuality: there is still a metainterface to the displaced interface.

The only question is whether and how the hidden interface levels and modes of *leiten* can be opened up. The discourse concerning the post-interface as well as the metainterface points to this challenge. For this is precisely the task of a critique of digitality: It seeks to track down and open up the manifold and interconnected interface levels as well as physical guidance and ideological conduction processes, thanks to which computers run, and by which they are determined and used for purposes, spread in a networked manner as well as embedded, and furthermore are destined to a momentum of their own with the reinforcement of sensors.

If, as I argue, the totality and distinctiveness of the conditions and consequences of electronic digital computers in all their forms depend on the interface levels and fields of *leiten* mentioned above, then this is where critique's starting point can also be located. My proposal, therefore, is to begin a critique of digitality with interface analyses.

The multi-layeredness as well as both the historical and technical connectedness of the terms interface and *leiten* offer a real advantage here, because they open a unique horizon of inquiry. The question of interfaces is aimed both at present, addressable conditions and processes of guiding which are obvious, (one instance being, as previously mentioned, on the touch screen of my smartphone), and at hidden processes (thanks to which, for example, the internet connections of my smartphone and its sensing modes function), and last but not least at the intricacy of the collaborative co-existence that they form.

The challenge and imposition of analytically addressing the phenomenon of digitality in its form of increasing computerisation is thus afforded an intentionally open method—or more precisely, mode of questioning—by such an approach. It consists of starting at one level of the interface complex in order to enquire from that point onwards about any associated further interfaces and processes of *leiten*.

A challenge thus becomes a method. It is precisely the complexity of the interface concept and its forms of conducting and guiding that challenges us to ask constantly about further, (as yet) undeveloped interface levels of the phenomenon we started with. Which interfaces are still in play? Which processes of *leiten* are still part of it?

This does not mean that all interface levels can be ascertained in this way. For this mode of questioning promises no complete insight or overview, no transparency, as if nothing were able to escape these questions. Rather, this approach leads precisely to that which eludes (my respective possibilities of analysis). It motivates inquiry into the connections between concealment and disclosure and can thus—mindful of the different interface levels and fields of *leiten*—also help to involve specifically other disciplines in their search for answers.

Thus, this question horizon and modality radically counters the immaterial parts of digitality. Already the conceptual history of the interface, its path from conductivity and fluidity to the human-computer interface, have broken away from the "myth of disembodiment in the digital" (Robben 2012, p. 20). The question of interfacing as activities of *leiten*, as programmatic processes of

2.6 Question Mode (Interface Analyses)

conducting and guiding, necessarily calls to mind the materiality of connections and the dependence on electricity.

This is all the more true when it comes to the workings of algorithms, which sometimes possess such magical connotations. Algorithms only become effective in switching and conducting, and are nothing other than (partial) steps of a computer's programme, "embodied in its current states" (Krämer 2003, p. 172). Algorithms and consumption of current are inseparable.

Processes of computerisation are therefore not only answers to the challenges of anthropogenic climate change, for example, in that smart cities reduce CO_2 emissions through "intelligent" traffic light control and traffic schemes, and online conferences replace business trips. At the same time, they are part of the problem. Laura U. Marks used the massive increase in the use of streaming platforms during the 2020 Corona Shutdown as an opportunity to perform some illustrative maths. She has estimated the footprint of the (in)famous Netflix miniseries *Tiger King*, which was streamed approximately 34,000,000 times in the USA in just ten days in March 2020. The total energy consumed was equivalent to "the electrical consumption of Rwanda in 2016" (Marks 2020).

A further example of the reality and materiality of processes of *leiten* concerns the question of interfaces, in the instance that automation of machine learning turns out in fact to to be "heteromation" (Ekbia and Nardi 2017), in other words when the supposedly autonomous action of computers is conducted under "sociotechnical conditions" (Mühlhoff 2019) and concretely by "clickworkers […] via a series of interfaces" (Kaerlein 2020, p. 53). As revealed in 2019, Amazon employs thousands of people around the world to listen in on what *Alexa* captures in order to improve its digital voice assistance. In the wake of these revelations, similar eavesdropping scenarios also emerged as common practice at Apple, Google, Microsoft, and Facebook (see Bodoni 2019). *Easy listening:* Workers review and annotate what is recorded and automatically transcribed to "eliminate gaps in Alexa's understanding of human speech" (Day et al. 2019). Here again, interface analysis could commence, investigating such processes of listening and typing.

Such an analysis could use concrete examples to address the relationship between *subface* and *surface,* beginning with simple, low-paying tasks, which allow the very development of an artificial intelligence that seems so far removed from humans. Because AI's invisible, supposedly human-independent, autonomous decision-making work, with which the immaterial magic of digitalicity continues to gain influence, is also based on its opposite. There is (human) interface work—at all levels—in development of this intelligence:

> This kind of invisible, hidden labor, outsourced or crowdsourced, hidden behind interfaces and camouflaged within algorithmic processes is now commonplace, particularly in the process of tagging and labeling thousands of hours of digital archives for the sake of feeding the neural networks. Sometimes this labor is entirely unpaid, as in the case of the Google's reCAPTCHA. In a paradox that many of us have experienced, in order to prove that you are not artificial agent, you are forced to train Google's image recognition AI system for free, by selecting multiple boxes that contain street numbers, or cars, or houses. (Crawford and Joler 2018).

Methods of automated image recognition raise similar questions. The European Union-funded project "iBorderCtrl", which is developing and testing an automated EU border protection system, is an example. Interface analysis on the hidden AI or ADM processes of facial recognition enacted by "iBorderCtrl" (cf. iBorderCtrl 2016a; O'Shea 2018; Wolfangel 2018), which aims to detect lies automatically at EU border controls, could start for instance already with instructional visuals: i.e. the training materials used to train the network in recognising patterns, and thus to evolve within the process. From here, the further, multi-layered interface processes of iBorderCtrl's concept architecture (cf. Fig. 2.4) would have to be interrogated. These processes enter registration information via the Traveller User Application (TUA), an app with a "traveller user interface", putting the data exchange with the iBorderCtrl database and the "Automatic Deception Detection System" (iBorderCtrl 2016a) into operation.

What is to be considered a face and what is to be considered a lie become as important as the procedure of attention with which

2.6 Question Mode (Interface Analyses)

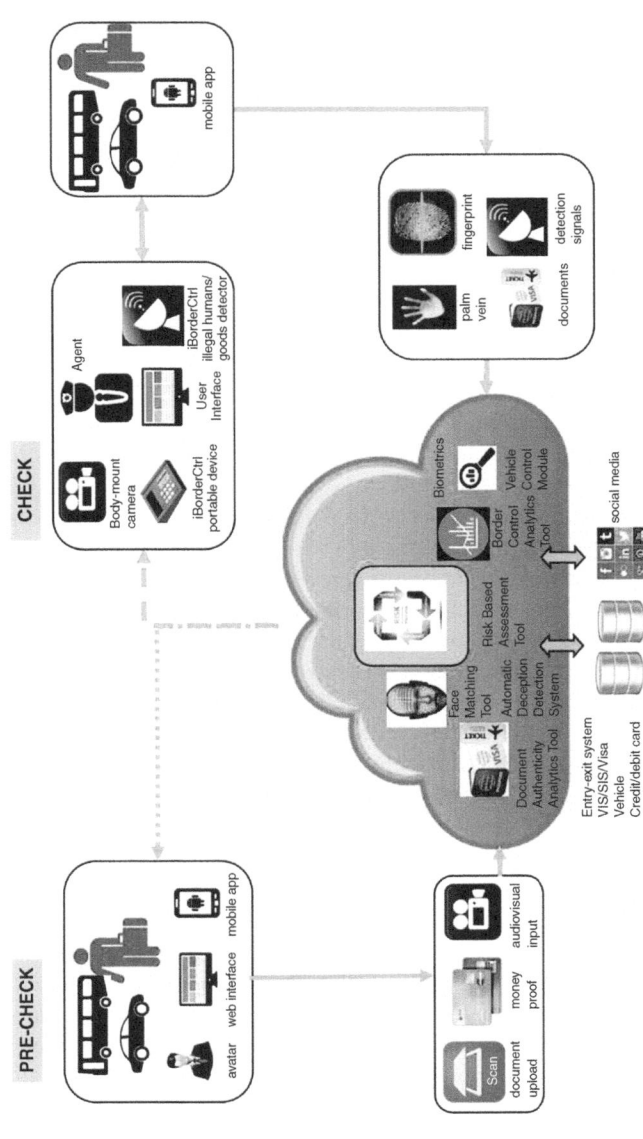

Fig. 2.4 iBorderCtrl: The (interface) layers of concept architecture (iBorderCtrl 2016b)

an AI or ADM system then analyses the selected visual material (cf. Gallagher and Jona 2019). For example, to investigate this relationship between training materials and algorithmic decision-making, Spectral Relevance Analysis (SpRAy), introduced in 2019, is a useful tool that is able to detect "a wide spectrum of learned decision behaviors" (Lapuschkin et al. 2019, p. 3) and render it visible through heat maps.

The apps used for the detection and control of the COVID-19 pandemic are also good examples of the urgency of interface analyses; both as a worldwide phenomenon, as "the global ecosystem of COVID-19 pandemic response apps" (Dieter et al. 2021), and in individual cases such as the German "Corona Data Donation App" already mentioned. Even the first two steps towards "identifying" a health scenario—the steps "Collect data" ("Daten sammeln") and "Transmit" ("Übermitteln")—exemplify just how interface processes follow one another and are interdependent (cf. RKI 2020b and Fig. 2.5).

The transition from step 1 ("Collecting data"), which relies on the sensory hardware interfaces of fitness wristbands and smartwatches and their related software, to step 2 ("Transmit"), in which "the collected data are pseudonymized and encrypted by the Robert Koch Institute", already highlights some precarious connections: Namely, the transition from sensory human machine interfaces and hardware-software interfaces of these wearables to the interface processes which transmit the data, after which point "novel algorithms" evaluate them (cf. Fig. 2.5). The questions of the functionality and effectiveness of these interface processes and who controls them are central both to the development of this app and to the harsh criticism of this application as "full monitoring" (Bock et al. 2020, p. 34).

One discipline that should be included here as part of a detailed analysis of tangible apps such as the "Traveller User Application" and the "Corona Data Donation" is the emerging *App Studies*. This emphatically empirical line of research, which since the late 2010s has combined approaches from science and technology studies, software studies, platform studies and infrastructure studies with cultural and media studies, involves "walkthrough" analyses of apps and their user interfaces (Light, Burgess, and Duguay

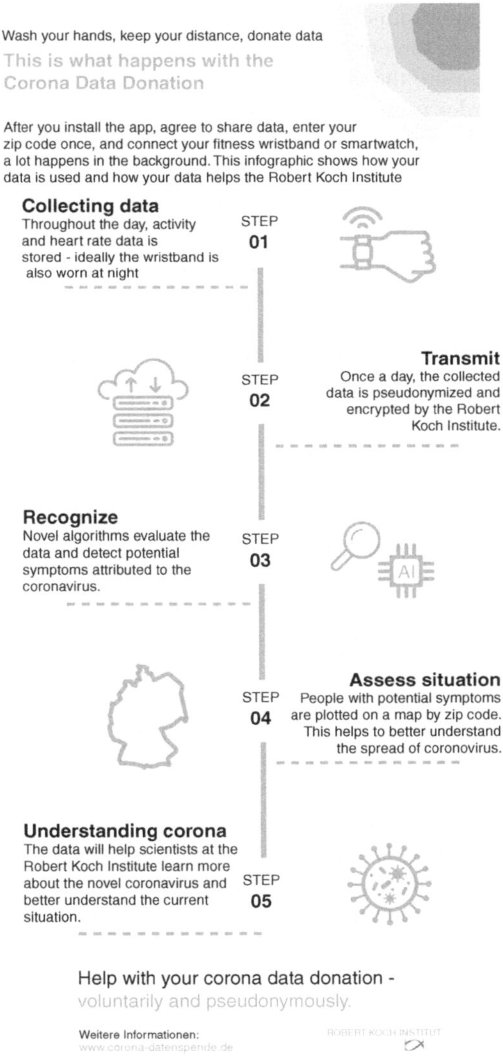

2.6 Question Mode (Interface Analyses)

Wash your hands, keep your distance, donate data
This is what happens with the
Corona Data Donation

After you install the app, agree to share data, enter your zip code once, and connect your fitness wristband or smartwatch, a lot happens in the background. This infographic shows how your data is used and how your data helps the Robert Koch Institute

Collecting data
Throughout the day, activity and heart rate data is stored - ideally the wristband is also worn at night

STEP 01

Transmit
Once a day, the collected data is pseudonymized and encrypted by the Robert Koch Institute.

STEP 02

Recognize
Novel algorithms evaluate the data and detect potential symptoms attributed to the coronavirus.

STEP 03

Assess situation
People with potential symptoms are plotted on a map by zip code. This helps to better understand the spread of coronovirus.

STEP 04

Understanding corona
The data will help scientists at the Robert Koch Institute learn more about the novel coronavirus and better understand the current situation.

STEP 05

Help with your corona data donation -
voluntarily and pseudonymously.

Weitere Informationen:
www.corona-datenspende.de

ROBERT KOCH INSTITUT

Fig. 2.5 "This is what happens ...": Translation for the infographics for the "Corona Data Donation App" of the German Robert Koch Institute (RKI 2020b)

2018). The aim of this "step-by-step observation and documentation of an app's screens, features and flows of activity" is to slow down and capture the everyday actions and interactions of using an app in order to use information gathered for critical analysis (ibid., p. 882).

To this end, Michael Dieter and Nathaniel Tkacz have distinguished the above-mentioned approaches as "digital cultural studies walkthrough", "data-centric walkthrough" and "'post-phenomenological' walkthrough" and from this have developed a "designerly walkthrough" (Dieter and Tkacz 2020), which makes partial perspectives of the other step-by-step analyses usable for the study of "banking apps". The walkthrough method is also used in Esther Weltevrede and Fieke Jansen's empirical analysis of dating apps. Here, it is complemented by further techniques such as "network sniffing" and "packet inspection", which help to identify ongoing network connections and data flows to third parties beyond the app provider and user (cf. Weltevrede and Jansen 2019). The analysis of the data flows, which are prepared specifically by the apps' application programming interfaces, provides information about a new data economy: Apps as "data objects" and their activities as "in-between brokers of data" (ibid.).

What is particularly interesting in this form of app studies for the further development of empirical interface analyses is the comparative analysis of graphical user interfaces (GUIs) and application programming interfaces (APIs). Weltevredes and Jansen's "comparative interface analysis" (ibid.) consists of comparing what data becomes accessible through the GUI (to me as the user) and what data becomes accessible through the API (to third parties). The relationship of these programmatic connections which pass on data is presented in the form of visualisations (cf. Figure 2.6). Using the example of the worldwide, popular dating app Tinder, a substantial imbalance in favour of the application programming interface becomes apparent.

Interface analyses—and this is what all these instances and examples boil down to—start from and move towards the complexity of interacting forms of *leiten* by engaging with one of

2.6 Question Mode (Interface Analyses)

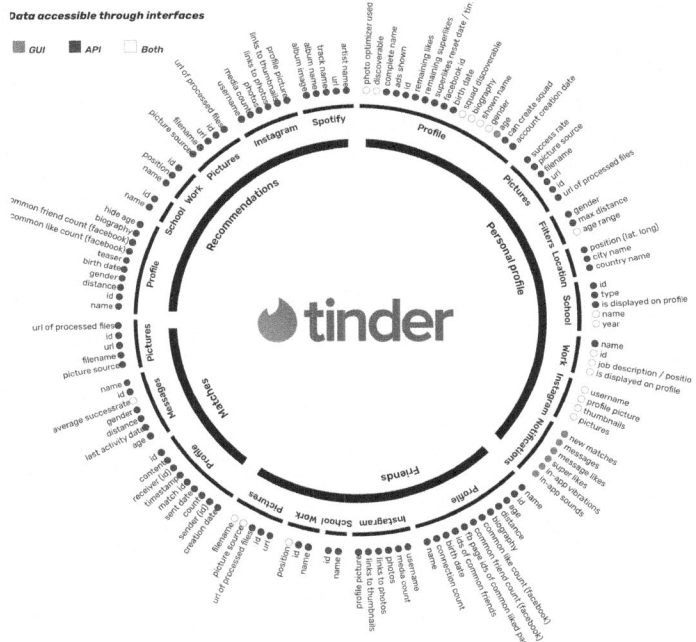

Fig. 2.6 The results of the comparative analysis of graphical user interfaces and application programming interfaces in the case of Tinder (Weltevrede and Jansen 2019)

these forms. They can begin where there is an offensive focus on depreatation and question, for example, the relationships between the mises-en-scène of user interfaces and the material as well as ideological conditions that make them effective. But they can also hitch on precisely at the point where user interfaces disappear.

Interfaces and processes of conduction and guidance, i.e. modes of *leiten*, are therefore not yet in themselves the answer to the question of what digitality and contemporary computerisation constitute or even mean. As a method, as a mode of questioning, however, the conceptual coexistence of the terms interface and *leiten* does offer an answer to the pressing complexity of this present scenario insofar as it, in turn, urges us to question the different levels of this complexity according to their respective relationships to one another. In other words, a critique of digitality can make use of the interface. Who begins where has thereby not yet been determined.

Programme and Everyday Life 3

3.1 Participation (Intermediate Spaces)

Digitality is a complex that involves me. Computerisation is a phenomenon in which I participate. Critique, for its part, calls for a double participation, which means exploring one's own interconnectedness, simultaneously inviting others to participate in the critical process.

My reflections so far have amounted to accepting and incorporating for critique the imposition that digitality, for a variety of reasons, constitutes. The reason why I have given a lot of space to the emphasis on these challenges is related both to the complexity described and to the idea of critique that are at stake here. Critique is not to be carried out in the manner of a judgment to be passed, and in the habitual gesture of an authority that presents conclusions from the detached position of having overcome. Instead, it seems to me as appropriate as it is helpful to approach the critique of digitality precisely from the difficulties it entails. For they lead to the numerous entanglements that are to be unfolded.

In order to develop an approach for such a critique that helps to open up the previously discussed complexity as a mode of questioning, I have placed the terms interface and *leiten* in new contexts. The questions about the different levels of interfaces and the fields of *leiten* allow interface analyses to be approached at every possible level: At the levels of hardware-hardware, hardware-software or software-software interfaces as well as at the levels of those interfaces that mediate between hardware/software constellations and that (non-computer) world to which we then may belong as users, as programmers and as objects of sensing procedures.

The final example, with which I would like to sketch a beginning of such an interface analysis, starts within this framework of hardware/software world relations, and I will use the smartphone and the interface processes that change with it as a point of departure. Starting from user interfaces, I will also question those levels and fields that elude (inter)active access when used but which, as I would like to show, are negotiated to a remarkable degree by that which offers itself for everyday use.

For this, the understanding of the established category of "user interface" must be expanded somewhat. Unidirectional use, at any rate, has long since had its day, and the process traditionally declared as *usability,* in which I consciously use computers for specific purposes, is today designed in such a way that my use is also helpful for the collection and evaluation of my data:

> By individuating us and also integrating us into a totality, their interfaces offer us a form of mapping, of storing files central to our seemingly sovereign—empowered—subjectivity. By interacting with these interfaces, we are also mapped: data-driven machine learning algorithms process our collective data traces in order to discover underlying patterns […]. (Chun 2013, p. 9).

Benefit has long been measured on both sides of the equation. *Using* is also *sensing* and *capturing.* Exactly this expansion of what used to be traded as usability is the first reason it seems both sensible and necessary to me to begin at this level.

In the second reason, the everydayness of digitality and computerisation coincides with the approach of understanding critique as a participatory unfolding of their concern. All over the world, people are involved to varying degrees in everyday digitality and its expansion as computerisation.

3.1 Participation (Intermediate Spaces)

Apart from the fact that the effects of computerisation reach in many ways even those who do not own devices—for example, in the form of economic, social and environmental consequences—the share of computer and internet use is continuously growing worldwide. In 2022, it was estimated that almost half of all private households had at least one computer, more than 6 billion people own smartphones, and more than 63% of the world's population use the internet (cf. Alsop 2022; DataReportal 2022; Statista Research Department 2022).

If these statistics allow us to speak of a "we" that deals with and benefit from concrete manifestations of digitality and its hidden processes everyday, then it is also we who are a mainstay of computerisation. We contribute to this process by procuring our devices and, through operating with them, by both pursuing our goals and at the same time doing our part of the work in capture capitalism. Our participation generates and (co-)decisively shapes the complex of digitality, and we share responsibility for its development. Thus already because of such common participation, it makes sense to start from where forms of digitality most obviously take place: In everyday interaction.

Addressing the manifestations and operations of human-computer(isation) interfaces therefore concurrently pursues the idea of critique posited here. As an unfolding of its concerns, the critique of digitality demands that we consider pro-actively our own participation through thoughts and actions—as an attempt at "conquest of freedom in our interlacements" (Garcés 2008) and our "de-automation" (Doll 2014, p. 246). To begin where digitality encounters us in our everyday lives, supports us and involves us in its processes (as well as in its progress), seems to me to be logical for the illustrative start of an interface analysis. It is an obvious starting point both in practical as well as theoretical terms.

Finally, the second form of participation that such a critique seeks to acknowledge likewise suggests to a begin in the customary, in the everyday. To enable that form of participation of others, this critique proposes, both in its rhetoric and in its systematics, to open up a discussion. In such arranged "arenas" (Latour 2004, p. 246) or, somewhat less spectacular and circus-like, "interstices" (Rouvroy 2013, p. 160), critique becomes an invitation to participate other than affirmatively. My proposal and example, therefore, is to use the everyday mannerisms enabled by interfaces as such an intermediate space, as a new and unintended turn of use.

What the mise-en-scène of such interfaces—now understood as new and doubly functional—can open up for a critique of digitality has already been addressed in the second chapter. Such mise-en-scène of conditional spaces of action simultaneously occlude and open up. In their still most common and dominant manifestation, i.e. graphical user interfaces, operational images come into play and both depresentatively fulfill and withdraw claims to power.

With these user interfaces, between commanding and complying, special interstices arise. In these intermediate spaces, I encounter ideas which conduct how my relationship as a human being to (such) programmed computer technology should be shaped, understood, and made tangible. Hence, in the aesthetics of command, something of those processes of digitality is revealed in which I am invited and called upon to participate, collaborate and also profit.

Using the aesthetic appearance of software (as interface mises-en-scène) for the development of critique, however, is not a new idea. Particularly since the mid-2010s, much has been published on this subject, particularly in German-language media studies (see also among others Hadler and Haupt 2016; Distelmeyer 2017; Ernst and Schröter 2017; Kaerlein 2018; Hadler and Soiné 2018, 2019; Wirth 2019). Furthermore already since the 1980s, works by Frieder Nake (2021/1986), Reinhard Budde and Heinz Züllighoven (1990), Cynthia and Richard Selfe (1994), Wendy Chun (2006), Alexander Galloway (2006), and Christian Ulrik Andersen and Søren Pold (2012) for example have all pointed towards this potential for a critique.

"Software tools unlock the object of our work, the programming material" and "thus become a cognitive tool," is a particularly optimistic formulation by the computer scientists Budde and

3.1 Participation (Intermediate Spaces)

Züllighofen (1990, p. 134). Their analysis of software systems used in companies leads them to the models that were the very basis of programming and now shape the industry in everyday use:

> It was only when we looked at the considerations expanded upon here that it became clear to us that, in the daily work of an office, enterprise *models of* a working context administered there have the same degree of reality for the office workers as the working situation administered by them has for those directly involved in it. (Budde and Züllighoven 1990, p. 135).

Their view of software tools as instruments of cognition, strongly influenced by Heidegger, provides a contrast to Kittler's critique of surface effects, although both positions can be combined in the concept of depresentation. It denotes the simultaneity of the possibilities of moving away from the hidden processes of internal telegraphy and returning to the unhidden processes of their tangibility and usability. In depresentation, computer technology becomes "concrete" (for humans) in the Kierkegaardian sense, as both movement between opposites and unfinished process (Kierkegaard 1983, p. 30; Distelmeyer 2017, pp. 31–32).

In negotiating human-computer(isation) interfaces, the underlying interface levels and fields of *leiten* remain obscured. However, precisely by means of their signals and modes of operation that invite user-participation, they can also be examined with regards to what is in fact not revealed here in terms of interfaces and processes of *leiten*, but which must nevertheless be in play (how?) in order for such interactions to take place successfully.

Our concrete participation in these processes is more than a context of delusion. It is more nuanced and therefore carries more responsibility than the role of mere subjects located within "interfacial regimes" (Bratton 2016, p. 229). We experience here more than just a form of domination that, in the sense of Giorgio Agamben's comparatively one-dimensional concept of the dispositif, produces unambiguous, planable effects of subjectivication (See also Agamben 2009; Distelmeyer 2017, pp. 51–64).

Graphical user interfaces, according to Benjamin Bratton (2016, p. 225) with reference to Agamben, "don't only mirror pre-existing user intentions; as whole interfacial regimes (such as Windows or iOS or Bloomberg Terminal, etc.), they also train thought toward certain ways of interpreting that environment through the repetition of represented interactions." However, as obviously as the mise-en-scène of interfaces seek to generate certain ideas in us as "users", these interface configurations are not just one-way streets of domination. Rather, they are interactive playgrounds of power. They involve me and create defined fields of action precisely by doing so. Thus—and here lies the central difference to Agamben's concept of the dispositive—they always offer the possibility for negotiation within the act of participation, which may elude the domination of the planned, and can then in turn result in unplanned outcomes. This in turn can be followed by recalibrations of the dispositive through a kind of "strategic completion" (Foucault 1980, p. 196) and perhaps even further unforeseen consequences.

Examples of interface mise-en-scène make digitality concrete in an illustrative and depresenting way. They simultaneously open up and close off, create proximity and distance in the way that they address "the user". However it is precisely this, their orientation towards "the user", that is becoming a waning preoccupation of computerisation. This is the third motivation for commencing my discussion with graphical user interfaces.

The developments of the Internet of Things, smart cities, new sensing technologies and, in particular, the accelerated momentum of computerisation through machine learning are designed to increase automation. Not only people, but computers, computer networks and the apparatuses they control are all at the centre of a multiplicity of transactions and layers of mediation. They have been for longer than we might realise. The the aforementioned high-frequency algorithmic trading processes, for example, developed between 2000 and 2006, continue to shape the development of global stock exchanges today (cf. Gresser 2018, pp. 10–11).

Even the data that the sensors on my smartphone collect about my movements and actions—and indeed the profile that can be

3.1 Participation (Intermediate Spaces)

derived from them—do not have to be (de-)presented to me in order to have any real impact on me. This step is technically unnecessary and its absence, i.e. the imperceptibility of data collection and analysis for equally hidden purposes, is, therefore, also a political issue.

That applies in particular to the decision-making processes used by artificial neural networks, which also present the developers of this form of algorithmic decision-making with the problem of only having the results of software procedures before them, ones that cannot be traced in any detail. The search for at least a retrospective breakdown of processes, a kind of algorithmic archaeology, is being conducted under the rubric of "Explainable AI" (See also Beuth 2018; Lapuschkin et al. 2019). AlgorithmWatch (2018) concludes that:

> Algorithmic decision-making (ADM) is a fact of life today; it will be a much bigger fact of life tomorrow. It carries enormous dangers; it holds enormous promise. The fact that most ADM procedures are black boxes to the people affected by them is not a law of nature. It must end.

The tendency of human-computer(isation) interfaces to no longer have to perform any arbitrary, obfuscating or goal-directed mediation work in the form of interface mise-en-scène, in order to nevertheless process "interaction", is taking on further forms. A barely futuristic part of this is the development of brain-computer interfaces or brain-machine interfaces (BMI), which are currently being promoted by Facebook and Elon Musk's company Neuralink. While Mark Zuckerberg's ideas of a "brain click"—of "typing with your mind" and of "allowing people to use their thoughts to navigate intuitively through augmented reality" (Cohen 2019)—are intended to work by means of electrodes placed on the scalp, Musk's Neuralink chooses the invasive approach (Musk and Neuralink. 2019): The insertion of electrodes into the cerebral cortex for reading brain activity and also, as Elon Musk explains, for "writing to the brain or stimulating neurons" (Neuralink 2020).

As early as 1945, Vannevar Bush (1945, p. 108) had suggested comparable ideas using "a couple of electrodes on the skull" in his famous essay, "As We May Think". Such older and newer visions of brain-computer interfaces strive for a technologically coupled immediacy. Thus, the interface complex can dispense with visual or acoustic (de-)presentations if such a cybernetic configuration can induce a direct flow of data, and a new intimacy.

The circumvention of the age-old compulsion to visualise—which since the implementation of graphical user interfaces in the mid-1980s coupled usability with comprehensibility—has long since exceeded such visions. As we may speak: Voice control, whose popularity was increasing by the end of the 2010s, especially in the use of smartphones and as voice assistance in living rooms and cars for example, celebrates new, and yet at the same time old, etiquettes.

Alexa! Hey Siri! The invocation is directed at voice interfaces, most of which are designed entirely "in the tradition of the servile female servant" (Angerer and Bösel 2015, p. 54), and which respond accordingly and submissively. "As an example, in response to the remark 'You're a bitch', Apple's Siri responded: 'I'd blush if I could'." (UNESCO 2019, p. 107) This occurs when two types of code appear to coincide: Those of human language and machine language.

Here the "Yes, Sir" principle of programmability is fulfilled as a clear announcement. Human and machine communication seem to become one, because my linguistic instruction becomes a command for the programmed machine without any visible or audible instance of intermediation. Software is no longer required to make such an appearance here. No depresenting signs interpose themselves conspicuously. I speak as "directly" (i.e. sensory mediated and algorithmically interpreted) as these so-called *natural user interfaces* behave "naturally" (i.e. modelled on "the human").

In this spirit, Till A. Heilmann describes a future in which voice input will become the predominant mode of interaction with digital computers. The "hitherto dominant interfaces of individual programmes, which have been primarily graphical and designed for keyboard, mouse, finger or gesture control" would thus be supplanted:

> Software, conceived as the sum of operating systems, application programmes, apps, online services, etc. used by informatic consumers, would thus be reduced to a collection of background functions that are largely 'invisible' to the user. Aesthetically it would merge into the "environment of everyday languages", to which it has so far been connected rather circuitously via keyboards, icons, pointing devices, programme windows, etc., and would ultimately become indistinguishable from them. (Heilmann 2018, p. 177)

The notion that computers could "finally morph into *black boxes*" (ibid.) by way of a direct bypass using speech recognition is important for a critique of digitality and the examples of common interface mises-en-scène I have chosen for discussion. This notion takes into account the potential decrease of depresentation. Of course, software would continue to exist as code running on hardware, but it would then "most likely lose its old form as an idiosyncratic surface phenomenon" (ibid.).

Thus significant changes are in the making: The interface mises-en-scène that make software visible as an idiosyncratic surface phenomenon by means of operational images are (also) now becoming historical phenomena. The wide-spread dominance of this form of depresentation—so common since the 1980s—may be slowly evaporating, and furthermore it is precisely because of this (also) historical dimension that I feel compelled to present my analysis of interfaces starting with graphical user interfaces.

For only as long as there is still a need for mediation, for software to be visible in a somehow comprehensible sense (i.e. as "enabling" input), does the afore-mentioned intermediate space exist: This interstice, with which—before it closes (while at the same time opening up anew on the inter-medial level of language and gesture)—critique can do something with it.

3.2 App Order (Objects and Processes)

When the iPhone was introduced in 2007, it marked the beginning of new mass participation in the process of computing. It was not then, of course, that the history of the smartphone began, which goes back to the 1990s, but the success story of "digital near-body technologies" took on a new form at this point as the mobile, full-fledged, networked and sensory computer that is still significant today (See also Kaerlein 2018, pp. 39–42). As a model for smartphones and tablet computers of various corporations, the iPhone established a relationship between humans and computer technology that relied on new processes of *leiten* (See also Fig. 3.1).

Two key features are pushed into the foreground here, not least through the iPhone's advertising materials: The capacitive touchscreen and the design of the graphical user interface operated by it. "In short," Pelle Snickars (2012, pp. 155–156) summarised by looking back at Lev Grossman's praise of the iPhone as "Invention of the Year" in 2007, "Apple's engineers used the touchscreen to sort of innovate past the GUI, which Apple once pioneered with the Mac, to create a whole new kind of interface, a tactile one that gives users the illusion of actually physically manipulating data with their hands."

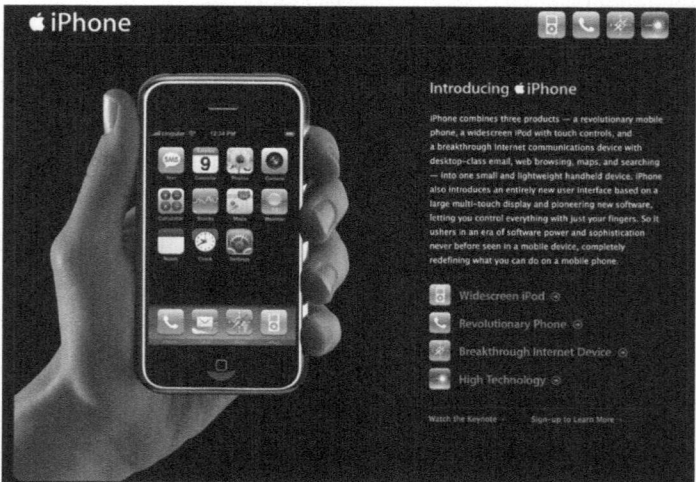

Fig. 3.1 New processes of *leiten*: The announcement of the iPhone in January 2007 at www.apple.com/iphone

3.2 App Order (Objects and Processes)

The touchscreen, no more an invention Apple than the graphical user interface, involves me in new ways in its fields of *leiten*. At the locations on these capacitive screens occupied by operational images, touch results in altered electrical capacities. A tactile act of conduction. By making use of the conductivity of my body, the relevant commands can be passed to the inner telegraphy of the computer to start, via hardware-software interfaces, the programme sequences that are attributed to each operational (and conducting and guiding) image. The previously cited illusion of physically manipulating data with one's hands is the product of a programming and hardware configuration that harnesses human bodies more aggressively than ever for the conduction of electrical impulses that run computers.

This leads to a remarkable contradiction. For it is precisely the touchscreen with its proactive and real-time impression of immediacy—"letting you control everything with just your fingers" (See also Fig. 3.1)—that invites us to think about processes of mediation. The promise of the user interface "with touch controls" (ibid.) demonstrates to the user's eyes and fingers what it is in this instance that interfaces are doing both concretely and also fundamentally: They conduct and guide, they enable processes of *leiten*.

Graphical user interfaces operate as a conduit for this interaction, where text-to-speech software can also announce what is displayed. This includes first and foremost, as access to the device's functions, a rasterised overview of programmes available, a kind of *app order*. An "order of choice" (Distelmeyer 2017, pp. 76–82) offers programmes directly on the homescreen, where the apps both allow and organise a "haptic experience of productivity" (Verhoeff 2012, p. 84).

In this context, apps are more than just programmes downloaded for mobile devices from central platforms such as the Mac App Store, the Galaxy Store, or the Huawei AppGallery. They need to be seen—as emphasised in the 2019 research agenda of empirical app studies—in their programmatic, operational, and infrastructural contexts, and also in their effects upon the status of software and suggested practices of use (See also Gerlitz et al. 2019). Apps both realise and mediate potentials for programmability.

Their manifestation—as illustrated by the ordering of apps on the homescreen of smartphones—is a radical shift. For it consists of the displacement of the demonstrative *object orientation* of the desktop (with its files and folders) by the *process orientation* of the homescreen (with its grid of apps). In fact, together with the touchscreen, this interface mise-en-scène represents nothing less than a decisive and enormously underestimated change in the idea of what people have to do with computers, an idea which was in dominance until 2007.

Thus, I would argue, a familiarisation with new conditions is facilitated through both a programmatic and—importantly—habitual process. One that trains us to understand the workings of computers less as actions that must emanate from me—as a subject with "user" status—rather than as permanently ongoing, quasi-natural processes of the *environmentalisation* of computer technology.

This aesthetic and logic mark an ostentatious and profound departure from the fundamental principle of graphical user interfaces that had been established since the mid-1980s. The interaction with the operational images of the desktop created and implemented at that time is emphatically object-oriented: Everything starts from the object. Steve Jobs had already copied this principle from innovations at Xerox PARC for the 1983 Apple Lisa (See Fig. 2.3). By pointing, selecting and clicking an object or file is highlighted with the mouse so that actions can be defined and performed upon them via either menu commands or the subsequent double-click (See also Fig. 3.2).

The conceptual closeness between object-oriented programming and object-oriented interaction has been summarised thus by Alan Kay (2001, pp. 129–130, my emphasis added), who has been responsible for promoting the development of both of these processes:

> *[O]bject oriented* means that the object knows what it can do. In the abstract symbolic arena, it means we should first write the object's name (or whatever will fetch it) and then follow with a message it can understand that asks it to do something. In the concrete user-interface arena, it suggests that we should select the

3.2 App Order (Objects and Processes)

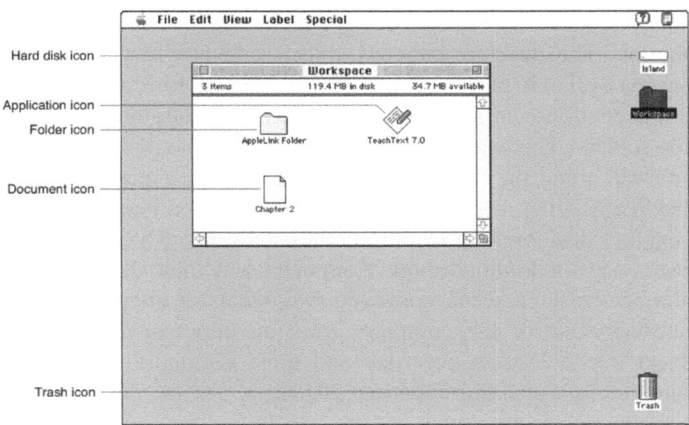

Fig. 3.2 Objects first: the object orientation by means of operational images ("icons") on the desktop, demonstrated in the *Macintosh Human Interface Guidelines* of 1992 (Apple Computer Inc. 1992, p. 224)

> object first. It can then furnish us with a menu of what it is willing to do. In both cases we have the *object* first and the *desire* second.

Accordingly, my use of the term "object orientation" refers neither strictly to object-oriented programming nor solely to object-oriented interaction. Instead, it is concerned with the commonality of the two practices emphasised by Kay and with both a paradigm and a particular way of thinking about computer programming and computer use. This model, in which "objects are the dominant structural elements", prevailed not least because, according to Gabriel Yoran (2018, pp. 124–125), it approximates the "everyday experience of objects".

Reinhard Budde and Heinz Züllighofen (1990, p. 229) have summarised this in terms of an "understanding of the design and use of software" as "object-oriented modeling". Objects, classes and class relations are as much a part of programming as the learned interaction in interface mises-en-scène, where "we do not depend on knowledge of the internal structure of objects to understand how to handle them" (ibid., p. 238).

In this sense, the desktop became the blockbuster of object orientation. The desktop gathered objects and provided access to them as well as to programmes that could likewise become objects in this environment alongside files as well as both in and alongside folders. This was a key to the success of the personal computer (PC) and the "popular computing" that it ushered in (See also Wirth 2019), which in turn formed the second major wave of computer development from the 1980s onwards. The object oriented way of thinking about computers and their use that this interface mise-en-scène conveyed was ideal for supporting the transformation of the computer from an impersonal hardware object into a PC, an everyday and most decidedly "personal" computer (see also Ehrmanntraut 2019).

Computer programmes and its "shifters, pronouns like 'my' and 'you,' that address you, and everyone else, as a subject" (Chun 2006, p. 21) worked to sustain this staging of objects and subjects. Interaction, commanding and complying, was and still is based on the interface mise-en-scène that orchestrates the behaviour of *my* digital objects.

However, it is exactly this that is reversed in the homescreen of the iPhone and all subsequent smartphones and tablet computers to this day—namely, into a *process-oriented* interaction. The operative images of this interface mise-en-scène no longer primarily depresent documents, files or folders, but programmes. Even their name has changed. In the *Macintosh Human Interface Guidelines,* there was still talk of both "program" and "application", with "application" defined as a "program that performs a specific task, such as word processing, database management, or graphics" (Apple Computer Inc. 1992, p. 363). In the *iPhone User Guide* (Apple Inc. 2008), on the other hand, the app—the "application" and its association with processes of application and use—has completely displaced the word "program" and any association with coded instruction. The new primacy of programmes is accompanied by a renaming that no longer evokes the process of programming itself.

The desktop dominance of files and folder structures, where programmes could also be found, is likewise reversed in the app homescreen. It gives way to the dominance of this new under-

3.2 App Order (Objects and Processes)

Fig. 3.3 Apps first: Screenshots of the first iPhone presentation (Apple Inc. 2007)

standing of programmes, where all that used to be files can now be found. Consequently I now require a new support in order to access what was previously visible as my digital objects on my desktop or in folders. This was exemplified by Steve Jobs in the first iPhone presentation in January 2007 (See also Fig. 3.3).

"With a little help from my friends": To find this song, you first have to select the designated programme in the homescreen, which not only plays music but also displays it straight away (as an operational image or character). No longer do data appear as interface objects of a desktop and folder system. Instead, they are part of a new programmatic and grid-oriented order: An interface mise-en-scène involving those apps that I now have to launch first in order to then search for the required digital objects in the programme now running—like *my* photos, music or notes for example. They exist (for me) only as programme items. With the apps of the homescreen, software becomes the first object of my interest or desire.

This interface mise-en-scène initiates a new way of dealing with computers. I align actions performed on my touchscreen with the grid of programmes whose flow I enter in order to find those objects within in it that had previously been the starting point of my actions. It wasn't until 2017, with the iOS 11 operating system, that the principle of object orientation would make a limited comeback through the appearance of the "Files" app. As one programme among many, that had already been introduced in Android operating systems in 2010 with the "My Files" app (See also Distelmeyer 2019, pp. 86–89).

Programmes are everything in this process-oriented (inter)action. Indeed programmes also appeared on the desktop, and nothing works on the desktop without the primacy of the programme; after all, even the desktop's file manager is nothing other than a running programme. It is only the gesture that is now different. *Process/programme first:* Initially, to the fore comes the mass and power of the programmes, which I can organise and select within the grid of the homescreen, but which I do not own, move and create in the previous and more familiar way as was the case with files and folders.

A new inventory. Given that my objects only show themselves under the conditions and in the course of the programme commanding them, the fundamental property of digital objects is brought to a head here, "with which we are interacting, and with which machines are simultaneously operating" (Hui 2016a, p. 48). I am therefore given to wonder what other significance the possessive pronoun "my" has in this scenario. Exactly whose possession is implied here? Whatever the case, I do not own these programmes, these commodities of the software industry; I merely acquire the right to their lawful use.

In contrast to the established concept of object orientation, which connects a programming paradigm with an interaction gesture, process orientation describes the programmatic change of this interaction gesture. It consists primarily in shifting attention away from digital objects and towards the processes of the programmes that make them appear.

I call this "process orientation" to indicate, in particular, the new importance of the environment of these objects, which is emphasised by the afore-mentioned shift. In computer science, a "process" is understood as "the entire information regarding the state of a running programme" (Mandl 2010, p. 66). The "process (also called task in some operating systems) provides the runtime environment for a programme on a computer system and is a dynamic sequence of actions with corresponding state changes" (ibid.).

The new relationship between object and environment, which foregrounds the programme within the context of process orientation—here regarded as a runtime environment—thus becomes a new framework of possibilities. In this framework, after entering the app's order of processes and with its touchscreen (pre)condition, a new way of dealing with digital objects also becomes possible: The supposedly "direct" manipulation of objects such as pictures and maps by *reaching in* with my fingers, which, thanks to their conductivity, conduct changes. Thus a solution to the problem of developing a graphical user interface for use on a small screen rapidly became a successful model, and soon not only for small screens.

3.3 Always on (Era of Software Power)

Process orientation is a shift of attention towards very specific processes, towards programmes and software. In the ordered grid of the apps, what underlies the functioning of programmes on smartphones technically is in a sense depresented: The principle of sandboxing can be understood as a form of software diversification, in which the diverse programmes do not access *all* stored data, but only the data assigned to them (See also Hagen 2018, pp. 75–79).

An oft-repeated rationale for isolating app data from other apps and the operating system is that it increases security. This limits "the potential for security breaches" (de Agonia 2017). A less prominent rationale is the resulting change in the status of software: It ideally supports the app business model, for which smartphones also provide the platforms. Apple advertised the iPhone in 2007 with the words that it marked the beginning of "an era of software power" (See also Ripley 2008, p. 91 and Fig. 3.1).

The new status of software unfolds on a number of interface levels, whose interaction enables the conductive mediation between body and computer, controlling 'everything with just your fingers' and not just limited to the internal telegraphy of my device. 'Everything' here also includes 'everything' that networking entails—programmes that require a connection to the internet. The question here as to what the capacitive touchscreen actually allows conductive contact with leads to questions concerning how internal and external telegraphy—the first and second fields of *leiten*—interact in the process.

The homescreen has in a way levelled out the different functional requirements. Apps for calculating tasks, for example, and word processing sit next to the "Weather", "Stocks" and "YouTube" app, which, in contrast to apps such as "Calculator" and "Notes", always require a running internet connection (see Fig. 3.1). This equal-ranking coexistence installs the *always-on* of these forms of mobile and permanently networked computers as a new matter of course in the user interface. The iPhone's historical status as role model therefore relates both to ideas of how a smartphone should look and function and of understanding computers as being *already* and *always* connected to the internet. Here, Sun Microsystems' advertising slogan from the early 1980s is being implemented as a new and fundamental philosophy: "The network is the computer."

This is today's everyday life—it is the basis of computerisation, its *sensing procedures* and also the function of artificial neural networks for voice and face recognition on smartphones. As an everyday experience, this *always-on* facilitates the equating of the "digital" with protocological networking. It reinforces the fourth imposition of digitality, and above all it allows computing processes to be increasingly outsourced. It no longer depends (only) on the computing power and storage capacity of my device. The connection to powerful internet services and hardware systems, programming and interface levels required for this are becoming more and more important.

This has quite literally far-reaching consequences for the status and power of software which will change significantly and fundamentally. For if software becomes the first object of my interest through the mise-en-scène of a process-oriented interface, it can spread decisively through the *always-on*. It shifts, as Irina Kaldrack and Martina Leeker (2015, pp. 9–10) have illustrated, from a product to a service:

> In the past, shrink-wrapped software, as it was called, had to be purchased, installed on a personal computer (PC), configured, and updated regularly. Today, however, it suffices to log on to a single

3.3 Always on (Era of Software Power)

> platform and install a service to easily access Dropbox, Facebook, Google, etc. In parallel to the development of clouds, web services, and mobile apps on the consumer market, 'classic' software providers are moving to subscription models in ever-greater numbers: Adobe Creative Suite becomes Adobe Creative Cloud and Microsoft Word becomes Office 365. Software is no longer purchased, but rather can be rented. [...] Ownership of software is thus becoming obsolete, replacing goods as property through service use.

Thus, another dimension of process orientation and the advertised "era of software power" unfolds. For such a programme to become usable on my computer, in addition to its interface processes between hardware and software, it also needs those of the external computers of an internet service, which in turn are mediated according to the TCP/IP software interface. Connections to the *cloud*—being "more a euphemism for a 'hidden bunker in Idaho or Utah'" (Morozov 2013, p. 25) rather than the celestial name of a ubiquitous availability—need to be built and regulated. Software spreads through networked, hardware and as a consequence the process, the runtime environment for the programme on my computer, now necessarily includes the runtimes of the internet, i.e. external computers.

So it becomes increasingly significant that my touching an operational (and conducting and guiding) image on the touchscreen does more than just guide the computational processes and energy consumption of my device. The act of launching (internet-based) apps becomes an entry into a flow that—and this is crucial to the idea of *capture capitalism*—no longer distinguishes between programme flow and network traffic. Signals and data flow, and for this purpose, the human body itself enters into the fields and processes of *leiten* that interfaces enable and require.

The *always-on* is therefore nothing other than a further turn towards (interface) processes. It gives additional contours to the process orientation that I encounter, at first glance, as an interface mise-en-scène, and the processes that become the environment here also include the procedures of the network connection.

Thus, the first two fields of *leiten* converge. While the fields of internal and external telegraphy continue to exist under their own conditions, they become indistinguishable however in the fourth field of *leiten* in which I handle the smartphone and provide input.

Making processes go: The interplay of touchscreen and process orientation, which as already mentioned has created a new standard since 2007, thus proceeds as technically as it does ideologically. It is, especially in its orientation towards the interface processes of permanent networking, a functional part of computerisation for which technical-physical processes of *leiten* are created and regulated. At the same time, and on precisely this basis, an ideological form of *leiten* emerges that is no less important for its functioning. It includes what is incorporated as a "user" and what can be excluded. It emerges, is needed and makes critique possible in that this form of *leiten* manifests itself as the depresenting appearance of those technical-physical processes with which—in order for it to run—it is operationally connected.

Seen in this light, the interface mise-en-scène of the process-oriented app order provokes both conclusions and questions that become highly sensitive against the background of some of the critiques of computerisation brought together in the first chapter. This applies in particular to considerations of *capture, sensing* and the possibilities of an *algorithmic governmentality* based on them.

This interface mise-en-scène introduces a new understanding of computers and commonises it in every sense. How people have to react with this technology here no longer emanates from them and their objects, which in turn may prompt further questions of ownership and purpose, but now emanates from processes that run always and everywhere in the spirit of digitalicity. What is staged and habitualised in this way is the *environmentalisation* of technology that computerisation (for us) is supposed to be.

There is much to be said for seeing this operational departure from the primacy of the object as also demonstrating the departure from the primacy of the subject. Thus, along with the object, the subject is also displaced, through which—as similarly posited by the theories of techno-ecology—becomes absorbed on an equal footing with its former object counterpart as "being in the control loop" in the exchange processes of the network (Hörl 2008, p. 646).

3.3 Always on (Era of Software Power)

This is made possible by the fact that the equal position of computers compared with their networks becomes commonplace; networks which, even more than my sealed but still present device, elude my observation and scrutiny, contributing towards the myth of immateriality. The strategic renaming of "Apple Computer Inc." to "Apple Inc." with which Steve Jobs brought his iPhone presentation to a pictorial close in 2007 (See also Kaerlein 2018, pp. 97–99) fits seamlessly into this logic." The computer" as we knew it before is to disappear quite literally.

Thus, to put it more succinctly, is the farewell to my data as property celebrated. My data now belong to the programmes that—*always on*—are already and at all times operating with them. The implicit requirement of capture capitalism and algorithmic governmentality to make my data available to programmes is made explicit here: It becomes commonplace by becoming a default setting for the use of mobile computers.

Though not always. For example, those who refuse to use cloud computing with Android operating systems will regularly receive a system notification with a warning. The German version reads: "Deine Daten werden nicht gesichert. Füge jetzt ein Sicherheitskonto hinzu." ("Your data is not saved. Add a security account now.") The "Save" operation, which in the context of the desktop means saving all data to the computer's hard drive, is suggested to be replaced here with backing up in the form of an input process into the external telegraphy of the cloud service. Data is now only safe when networks act on it.

Here, concepts of value are transformed into algorithmic operations of conducting and guiding, into operations of *leiten*, that make these concepts a reality by offering certain elements of participation. What it should consist of—returning briefly to the prime example of this development that extends far beyond individual corporations—was articulated very clearly by Steve Jobs in his last presentation on the iCloud network service in 2011. Promoting this next step of protocological automation he announced the establishment of a new centre, new processes, and new relationships, which combined outline the direction of ongoing computerisation as reaching far beyond iCloud:

> We're going to move the digital hub, the center of your digital life, into the cloud. Because all these new devices have communications built into them, they can all talk to the cloud whenever they want. And so now, if I get something on my iPhone it's sent up to the cloud immediately. Let's say I take some pictures with it, those pictures are in the cloud, and they are now pushed down to my devices completely automatically. And now everything's in sync with me not even having to think about it. I don't even have to take the device out of my pocket. [...] And so everything happens automatically and there's nothing new to learn. (Apple Inc. 2011).

This human-computer(ising) relationship has already been initiated, I conclude, by the interface mise-en-scène introduced in 2007. Its techno-logic, which governs purposes of computer(isation), is as follows: The *centre of my digital life* is neither me nor my computer. The centre is data streaming processes. It is a programme-controlled, protocological network of computers whose prescribed momentum simultaneously frees me up, is at my service, records my data at all times and holds it in a permanent process of transfer and evaluation. At the centre, to use the words of Manuel Castells' (2010, p. 500) critique of the network society, is "the power of flows".

I can participate consciously in these processes at any time. However I no longer have to. And yet my data still becomes part of this process regardless. Furthermore the consequences of these processes can still reach me personally be it, for example, via the synchronisation of my devices, as a simplification in the form of election advertising tailored to me, or in the form of a rejection from a job application process as a result of AI or ADM systems analysing and classifying patterns in my submitted data profile as unsuitable.

This is, of course, not without its contradictions. Companies and programmes continue to address me as an individual, invoking the You of "N(YOU) Media" (Chun 2016, p. 16) going on nevertheless to classify my data as part of a larger whole, a new programme-led plurality with Big Data's grids of similarity. And paradoxically, the displacement of the subject from the *centre of one's digital life* is also accompanied by a reintegration of the individual's body thus:

3.3 Always on (Era of Software Power)

With my finger, which operates the touchscreen and unlocks devices via a fingerprint; with my eye, which the iris scanner checks for authorisation; or with my face, of which recognition processes such as "Face ID" (Apple), "Face Recognition" (Samsung) or "3D Face Unlock" (Huawei) form their own picture with the aid of artificial neural networks (See Fig. 3.4).

It is precisely the new standard of unlocking the use of smartphones and tablets through facial recognition that can be understood as highly contradictory. The smartphone's departure from the object and its subject, with which the gesture of the personal (the PC) shifts to the processual of the network (i.e. the "centre of your digital life"), is counteracted by the sensory functions of the computer on the one hand, in that I am identified by my face. It depends on me, after all. On the other hand, however, this sensory detection by an ever-alert technology that also recognises me without being asked is furthermore a deepening of the process-oriented shift towards the concept of the "active network".

Perhaps it is something like this: It is not me who "recognises" this computer as mine, a device that secures my data as a *personal computer,* rather the computer within the network context "recognises" *me* so that it grants me access to this context, the new centre. The Huawei slogan "Unlock life's possibilities with 3D face unlock" (See also Fig. 3.4) seems to address this process precisely: It is to do with quite different possibilities of (digital) life than unlocking a or even "my" device.

Fig. 3.4 Unlocking possibilities: Huawei advertisement for "3D Face Unlock" (Krishnan and Hal 2018)

Here, a connection could be sought between the process orientation and the "technotronic regime" (Mbembe 2017, p. 24), in which "imprints (fingerprints, scans of the iris and retina, forms of vocal and facial recognition) make it possible to measure and archive the uniqueness of individuals". The fact that such measuring and archiving allows a new, "(a) normative" power to be developed vis-à-vis these individuals—in the sense that *datamining* based on their "statistical doubles" promotes a quasi-automatic shaping of futures—is the subject of the critique of algorithmic governmentality (See also Rouvroy and Berns 2013). Thus, it can also draw momentum from how smartphones or tablets with touchscreens and app order are used in everyday life.

The empirical approaches of app studies lend themselves to detailed analyses of how processes of governing and *leiten* take place via concrete apps and "an app's governance", i.e. "how the app provider seeks to manage and regulate user activity" (Light/Burgess/Duguay 2018, p. 890). In this context, the historical transition from object to process orientation becomes highly relevant especially for the walkthrough method of analysing user interfaces and the relationships between technical (infra-)structure and its use embedded therein.

This transition provides the techno-logical precondition for this by positioning the relationship between humans and computer(isation) on a new footing. As a "haptic experience of productivity" (Verhoeff 2012, p. 84), process-oriented logic puts a new relationship to data in my hands, which increasingly and habitually accommodate concepts of the data economy as examined in app studies. The unequal relationship between the amounts of data made available via graphical user interfaces to me as a user and via application programming interfaces to third parties—thus making apps "in-between brokers of intimate data" (Weltevrede and Jansen 2019)—is preceded by both the introduction of a process-oriented interface mise-en-scène and its departure from data as ownership-indicating goods. The programmatic app order of touchscreens is the ideal precondition for this: It is both the technical and ideological environment and condition of these new data objects and their economy.

3.4 No Conclusion (Mistrust and Decision-Making)

From his discussion of computerisation, Dirk Baecker (2018a, p. 259) has derived a design task. The "challenge facing the design of the next society", he argues, consists in making the increasingly invisible processes of linking heterogeneous processes "in the medium of algorithmic connectivity" visible "and keeping them available for intervention". This intervention, which "shows what can no longer be labelled or designated", is intended to have the effect that "we may at least rely on being able to become suspicious" (ibid., p. 260).

As important as such a new aesthetic is, the possibility of a similar intervention, albeit from another side, already exists to a not inconsiderable degree. It is because processes of depresenting, making visible and keeping available permanently occur that a critique of digitality is always and already able to become suspicious of any interface mise-en-scène. The interstices in which critique can begin and requires additional unfolding are opening up on a daily basis by way of our dealings with that which makes us the active "we" of digitality and computerisation. The interventionist's responsibility does not only lie here in the field of design and programming with its shifting boundaries of revealing and depresentation. It lies also in the interface terrains of everyday life in which all participants can gather.

As participants we can decide to use both the appearance and behaviours of computerisation as an invitation and scope for critique. This requires that we break with both our traditional (mis) understanding of tools and tendency to underestimate the interface-complex. In this way, the procedures of digitality can become the very entry point into procedures of a critique that asks about interface levels and fields of *leiten*.

There are of course limits to this. The fact that it is not possible to simply deduce or detect the depths of hidden interface levels and processes of *leiten*, of protected programmes and algorithms designed and constructed by leading corporations and government technologies, or of unseen computational steps of an AI or

ADM system and even data transfer between platforms, all amounts to problems that such lines of enquiry will inevitably encounter. This is certainly already the case with the example of the smartphone, which I could only touch upon in this chapter.

The illustrative limitations of this method of critique also testify to a larger problem: The lack of possibilities for insight and voice in the advancement of computerisation. This issue poses a very real challenge to societies and especially to democracies.

This particular challenge arises from the fact that the non-observability of procedures is supposed to guarantee automatic, or more precisely, programmable processes. For it is precisely this—the potentially infinite number of definable automatisms—which is treated as the advantage of ongoing computerisation. However it is simultaneously precisely this arrangement of programmatic automatism, whose principles lie hidden, that stands in direct opposition to the ideal of democracy, one which indeed upholds negotiability and comprehensible processes of decision-making. How this contradiction is to be resolved remains the most difficult and still open question in managing digitality.

Interface analyses can already help sensitise us to this question insofar as they encounter necessarily the decisive programmability that distinguishes computer technology from all other forms of the technical. It is decisive as a matter of principle, since it becomes functional based on decision logic and formalised orders and chains of command. It is decisive concretely since I encounter programmability in my interactions with computers as results of such programmatic flexibilities and operational automatisms of switching and *leiten*. What I encounter in interface analyses—be it whether I start with the training materials for artificial neural networks or common graphical user interfaces—are effects of a programming that has already been decided.

It is precisely in the moments in which I programme (on the basis of programme sequences defined for such as purpose) or in which programming perceptibly changes that programmability can be experienced as something decisive. The change from object- to process-oriented interaction is just as much an example of this as the "Facebook Demetricator". Changes and rearrange-

3.4 No Conclusion (Mistrust and Decision-Making)

ments in what is customary make any order appear less self-evident.

This, then, could be a particular advantage of interface analyses for a critique of digitality: The examination of the forms of manifestation and effect of decisive programmability can help us recognise more clearly the political dimensions inherent in the advancement of computerisation. For it consists not only in concrete infrastructures, networks, platforms, data flows, forms of interaction, devices and (self-learning) programmes, but also in the principle of programmatic decidability and automation. Whether societies become programmed and programmable in this sense will therefore be decided by how the ambit of digitality is decided.

References

Adelung, Johann Christoph. 1808. *Grammatisch-kritisches Wörterbuch der Hochdeutschen Mundart. Zweiter Teil, von F–L*. Wien: Anton Pichler.

Agamben, Giorgio. 2009. *"What is an apparatus?" and other essays*. Stanford: Stanford University Press.

Aigner, Anton. 2011. *Die Kunst des Leitens. Erfahrungen–Einsichten–Hinweise*. Würzburg: Echter.

Alfter, Brigitte, Ralph Müller-Eiselt, and Matthias Spielkamp. 2019. Introduction. In *Automating society. Taking stock of automated decision-making in the EU*, ed. Matthias Spielkamp, 6–12. Berlin: AlgorithmWatch.

AlgorithmWatch. 2018. *The ADM manifesto*. https://algorithmwatch.org/en/the-adm-manifesto/.

Alsop, Thomas, Computer penetration rate among households worldwide 2005–2022, https://www.statista.com/statistics/748551/worldwide-households-with-computer/ (2022).

Amazon Instant Video Germany GmbH (Amazon). 2017. You are wanted. *Facebook-Post vom* 6 (7): 2017. https://www.facebook.com/watch/?v=1917119448533626.

Amnesty International. 2016. *"This is what we die for": Human rights abuses in the Democratic Republic of the Congo power the global trade in cobalt*. London: Amnesty International.

Andersen, Christian Ulrik, and Søren Pold, eds. 2012. *Interface criticism. Aesthetics beyond buttons*. Aarhus: Aarhus University Press.

———. 2018. *The Metainterface. The art of platforms, cities and clouds*. Cambridge: MIT Press.

Andreas, Michael, Dawid Kasprowicz, and Stefan Rieger. 2018. Unterwachen und Schlafen: Einleitung. In *Unterwachen und Schlafen: Anthropophile Medien nach dem Interface*, ed. Michael Andreas, Dawid Kasprowicz, and Stefan Rieger, 7–31. Lüneburg: Meson Press.

Angerer, Marie-Luise, et al. 2018. Sensing. The knowledge of sensitive media. http://www.sensing-media.de/en/sensing-en/.

Angerer, Marie-Luise, and Bernd Bösel. 2015. Capture all, oder: Who's afraid of a pleasing little sister? *Zeitschrift für Medienwissenschaft* 13: 48–56.

APA. 2019. Forscher entwickeln "High-Tech-Bienenstock" mit Robotern als Boten. *Der Standard* 08 (04): 2019. https://www.derstandard.de/story/2000101028274/forscher-entwickeln-high-tech-bienenstock-mit-robotern-als-boten.

Apple Computer Inc. 1983. Apple LISA Computer–VIDEO DEMO–7/Jan/1983. https://www.youtube.com/watch?v=wbO-vY9tbNY&t=10s.

———. 1992. *Macintosh human Interface guidelines*. Reading: Addison-Wesley.

Apple Inc. 2007. iPhone keynote. https://www.youtube.com/watch?v=H3uaJIaIArs.

———. 2008. iPhone user guide for iPhone and iPhone 3G. https://www.manualsdir.com/manuals/47955/apple-iphone_iphone-3g-user-manual.html.

———. 2011. WWDC 2011. https://www.youtube.com/watch?v=LPMjUtfQPks.

Arlt, Hans-Jürgen, Martin Kempe, and Sven Osterberg. 2017. *Die Zukunft der Arbeit als öffentliches Thema. Presseberichterstattung zwischen Mainstream*. Frankfurt a. M: Otto Brenner Stiftung.

Arora, Siddharth et al. 2014. High-accuracy discrimination of Parkinson's disease participants from healthy controls using smartphones. *IEEE International Conference on Acoustics, Speech and Signal Processing* (Proceedings), 3641–3644.

Ash, James, et al. 2017. Unit, vibration, tone: A post-phenomenological method for researching digital interfaces. *Cultural Geographies* 25 (1): 165–181.

Ash, James. 2015. *The Interface envelope. Gaming, technology, power*. New York: Bloomsbury.

Baecker, Dirk. 2018a. *4.0 oder Die Lücke die der Rechner lässt*. Leipzig: Merve.

———. 2018b. Neue Wetten auf Komplexität. *Festival Next Level* 2018: 1–7. https://catjects.files.wordpress.com/2018/11/neue_wetten.pdf.

Bär, Dorothee. 2020. Ich hoffe, dass wir auch digital alle gestärkt aus der Krise kommen. *Der Spiegel* 30 (03): 2020. https://www.spiegel.de/politik/deutschland/dorothee-baer-ich-hoffe-dass-wir-alle-aus-der-krise-auch-digital-gestaerkt-kommen-a-ed95eacf-3a93-4a06-8e23-1fd995305137.

Barthes, Roland. 1977. *Image music text. Essays selected and translated by Stephen Heath*. London: Fontana Press.

———. 2013. *Mythologies*. New York: Hill and Wang.

Bauer, Nora. 2017. Sonne, Mond und Sterne. *Deutschlandfunk* (Ursendung: 29.04.2017). https://player.fm/series/feature-deutschlandfunk-kultur-2466450/sonne-mond-und-sterne-uberwachung-durch-strassenlaternen.

References

Benjamin, Walter. 2010. *Über den Begriff der Geschichte (Werke und Nachlaß. Kritische Gesamtausgabe 19)*. Berlin: Suhrkamp.

Bennett, Andy. 2014. *Mediated youth cultures: The internet, belonging and new cultural configurations*. London: Palgrave.

Beuth, Patrick. 2018. Wie tickt eine künstliche Intelligenz? *Der Spiegel* 15 (06): 2018. https://www.spiegel.de/netzwelt/web/explainable-ai-auf-der-cebit-2018-wie-tickt-eine-kuenstliche-intelligenz-a-1213016.html.

Bexte, Peter. 2002. Kabel im Denkraum. In *Updates. Visuelle Medienkompetenz*, ed. Arthur Engelbert and Manja Herlt, 17–43. Würzburg: Königshausen & Neumann.

Bharthur, Deepti. 2020. The valley and the virus. *Bot Populi* 03 (04): 2020. https://botpopuli.net/big-tech-covid19-corona-silicon-valley.

Biselli, Anna and Martin Tschirsich. 2020. Die Datenspende-App braucht mehr Transparenz. *netzpolitik.org*. https://netzpolitik.org/2020/die-datenspende-app-braucht-mehr-transparenz/.

Blum, Andrew. 2019. *Tubes: A journey to the center of the internet*. New York: HarperCollins.

Boast, Robin. 2017. *The machine in the ghost: Digitality and its consequences*. London: Reaktion.

Bock, Kirsten, et al. 2020. Datenschutz-Folgenabschätzung für die Corona-App. *Forum InformatikerInnen für Frieden und gesellschaftliche Verantwortung (FIfF)* 14 (04): 2020. https://www.fiff.de/dsfa-corona-file/at_download/file.

Bodoni, Stephanie. 2019. Facebook quizzed by watchdog for listening to users' chats. *Bloomberg* 14 (08): 2019. https://www.bloomberg.com/news/articles/2019-08-14/facebook-quizzed-by-privacy-watchdog-for-listening-to-user-audio.

Boellstorff, Tom. 2014. Die Konstruktion von Big Data in der Theorie. In *Big Data. Analysen zum digitalen Wandel von Wissen, Macht und Ökonomie*, ed. Rámon Reichert, 105–131. Bielefeld: transcript.

Boyd, Danah, and Kate Crawford. 2012. Critical questions for big data information. *Communications Society* 15 (5): 662–679.

Brand, Stewart. 1987. *The media lab. Inventing the future at MIT*. New York: Viking Penguin.

Bratton, Benjamin. 2016. *The stack: On software and sovereignty*. Cambridge: MIT Press.

Breljak, Anja, and Rainer Mühlhoff. 2019. Was ist Sozialtheorie der Digitalen Gesellschaft? Einleitung. In *Affekt Macht Netz. Auf dem Weg zu einer Sozialtheorie der Digitalen Gesellschaft*, ed. Anja Breljak, Rainer Mühlhoff, and Jan Slaby, 7–34. Bielefeld: transcript.

Bridle, James. 2018. *New dark age. Technology and the end of the future*. London: Verso.

Brockman, John. 2019. Der Geist der unbegrenzten Möglichkeiten. Von Kybernetik, Mensch und Maschine–eine kurze Geschichte des Nachdenkens über künstliche Intelligenz. *Süddeutsche Zeitung*, 11.

Bucher, Taina. 2018. *If... then: Algorithmic power and politics.* Oxford: Oxford University Press.

Budde, Reinhard, and Heinz Züllighoven. 1990. *Software-Werkzeuge in einer Programmierwerkstatt: Ansätze eines hermeneutisch fundierten Werkzeug- und Maschinenbegriffs.* München/Wien: Oldenbourg.

Bundesministerium für Gesundheit (BMG). 2020. *Erklärung von Kanzleramtsminister Helge Braun und Bundesgesundheitsminister Jens Spahn zur Tracing-App.* https://www.bundesgesundheitsministerium.de/presse/pressemitteilungen/2020/2-quartal/tracing-app.html.

Bundesministerium für Verkehr und digitale Infrastruktur (BMVI). 2017. *5G-Strategie für Deutschland. Eine Offensive für die Entwicklung Deutschlands zum Leitmarkt für 5G-Netze und -Anwendungen.* Berlin: BMVI.

Bundesministerium für Wirtschaft und Energie (BMWi). 2014. *Zukunft der Arbeit in Industrie 4.0.* Berlin: BMWi.

Bundesregierung. 2014. *Digitale Verwaltung 2020. Regierungsprogramm 18. Legislaturperiode.* Berlin: Bundesministerium des Innern.

———. 2018. *Digitalisierung gestalten. Umsetzungsstrategie der Bundesregierung.* Berlin: Presse- und Informationsamt der Bundesregierung.

Bush, Vannevar. 1945. As we may think. *The Atlantic Monthly* 176: 101–108.

Butler, Judith. 2006. What is critique? An essay on foucault's virtue. *transversal* 8, https://transversal.at/transversal/0806/butler/en.

Caliskan, Aylin, Joanna Bryson, and Arvind Narayanan. 2017. Semantics derived automatically from language corpora contain human-like biases. *Science* 356: 183–186.

Castells, Manuel. 2010. *The rise of the network society.* 2nd ed. Malden/Oxford: Wiley-Blackwell.

Catlow, Ruth, et al., eds. 2017. *Artists re:thinking the blockchain.* Liverpool: Liverpool University Press.

Chun, Wendy Hui Kyong. 2004. On software, or the persistence of visual knowledge. *Grey Room* 18: 26–51.

———. 2006. *Control and freedom. Power and paranoia in the age of fiber optics.* Cambridge: MIT Press.

———. 2013. *Programmed visions. Software and memory.* Cambridge: MIT Press.

———. 2016. *Updating to remain the same habitual new media.* Cambridge: MIT Press.

———. 2018. Queerying Homophily. In *Pattern Discrimination*, ed. Clemens Apprich, Wendy Hui Kyong Chun, Florian Cramer, and Hito Steyerl, 59–97. Lüneburg: Meson Press.

———. 2021. *Discriminating data. Correlation, neighborhoods, and the new politics of recognition.* Cambridge: MIT Press.

Cohen, Noam. 2019. Zuckerberg wants Facebook to build a mind-reading machine. *wired.* https://www.wired.com/story/zuckerberg-wants-facebook-to-build-a-mind-reading-machine/.

References

Conrad, Michael. 1988. The price of programmability. In *The universal Turing machine: A half-century survey*, ed. Rolf Herken, 285–307. Oxford: Oxford University Press.

Cook, Gary. 2017. *Clicking clean: Who is winning the race to build a green internet?* Washington: Greenpeace.

Couldry, Nick, et al. 2018. Media, communication and the struggle for social progress. *Global Media and Communication* 14 (2): 173–191.

Coy, Wolfgang. 1994. Aus der Vorgeschichte des Mediums Computer. In *Computer als medium*, ed. Norbert Bolz, Friedrich Kittler, and Christoph Tholen, 19–37. München: Fink.

Cramer, Florian, and Matthew Fuller. 2008. Interface. In *Software studies: A lexicon*, ed. Matthew Fuller, 149–152. Cambridge: MIT Press.

Crawford, Kate. 2021. *Atlas of AI. Power, politics, and the planetary costs of artificial intelligence*. New Haven: Yale University Press.

Crawford, Kate, and Vladan Joler. 2018. Anatomy of an AI system: The Amazon Echo as an anatomical map of human labor, data and planetary resources. *AI Now Institute and Share Lab* 07 (09): 2018. https://anatomyof.ai.

Cubitt, Sean. 2016. Digital aesthetics. In *A companion to digital art*, ed. Christiane Paul, 265–280. Chichester/Malden: Wiley-Blackwell.

D64 et al. 2020. Offener Brief: Geplante Corona-App ist höchst problematisch. *Chaos Computer Club* 24 (04): 2020. https://www.ccc.de/de/updates/2020/corona-tracing-app-offener-brief-an-bundeskanzleramt-und-gesundheitsminister.

DataReportal, Digital around the world, https://datareportal.com/global-digital-overview (2022).

Day, Matt, Giles Turner, and Natalia Drozdiak. 2019. Amazon workers are listening to what you tell Alexa. *Bloomberg* 11 (04): 2019. https://www.bloomberg.com/news/articles/2019-04-10/is-anyone-listening-to-you-on-alexa-a-global-team-reviews-audio.

de Maizière, Thomas. 2016. Datenpolitik im Spannungsfeld zwischen Schutzinteressen und Datenverwertung. *Alle Reden*, ed. Bundesministerium des Innern, für Bau und Heimat. https://www.bmi.bund.de/SharedDocs/reden/DE/2016/11/10ter-it-gipfel.html.

de Vaujany, François-Xavier et al. 2019. Communities versus platforms: The paradox in the body of the collaborative economy. *Journal of Management Inquiry* 1–18. https://doi.org/10.1177/1056492619832119.

de Agonia, Michael. 2017. How to use the files app in iOS 11. *Computerworld* 28 (07): 2017. https://www.computerworld.com/article/3211487/how-to-use-the-files-app-in-ios-11.html.

Dean, Jodi. 2008. Communicative capitalism: Circulation and the foreclosure of politics. In *Digital media and democracy. Tactics in hard times*, ed. Megan Boler, 101–122. Cambridge: MIT Press.

Dieter, Michael, and Nathaniel Tkacz. 2020. The patterning of finance/security: A designerly walkthrough of challenger banking apps. *Computa-

tional. Culture: 7. https://computationalculture.net/the-patterning-of-finance-security/.

Dieter, Michael, Anne Helmond, Nathaniel Tkacz, Fernando van der Vlist, and Esther Weltevrede. 2021. Pandemic platform governance: Mapping the global ecosystem of COVID-19 response apps. *Internet. Policy Review* 10 (3). https://doi.org/10.14763/2021.3.1568.

Distelmeyer, Jan. 2012. *Das flexible Kino. Ästhetik und Dispositiv der DVD & Blu-ray*. Berlin: Bertz + Fischer.

———. 2015. Digitalisieren. In *Historisches Wörterbuch des Mediengebrauchs*, ed. Heiko Christians, Matthias Bickenbach, and Nikolaus Wegmann, 162–178. Köln: Böhlau.

———. 2017. *Machtzeichen. Anordnungen des Computers*. Berlin: Bertz + Fischer.

———. 2018. Drawing connections: How interfaces matter. *Interface Critique Journal* 1: 22–32.

———. 2019. From object to process. Interface politics of networked computerization. In *After the post-truth (Artnodes, Nr. 24)*, ed. Jorge Luis Marzo Pérez, 83–90. Barcelona: Universitat Oberta de Catalunya.

Doll, Martin. 2014. Kritik als 'Befreiung des Denkens': Foucaults Politik der Entautomatisierung. In *Entautomatisierung*, ed. Annete Bauerhoch et al., 229–250. Paderborn: Fink.

Dracklé, Dorle. 2014. Medienethnologie/Medienethnographie. In *Handbuch Medienwissenschaft*, ed. Jens Schröter, 393–404. Stuttgart/Weimar: Metzler.

Drucker, Johanna. 2014. *Graphesis: Visual forms of knowledge production*. Cambridge: Harvard University Press.

Ehrmanntraut, Sophie. 2019. *Wie Computer heimisch wurden. Zur Diskursgeschichte des Personal Computers*. Bielefeld: transcript.

Ekbia, Hamid R., and Bonnie A. Nardi. 2017. *Heteromation, and other stories of computing and capitalism*. Cambridge: MIT Press.

Eckert, Werner. 2018. Faktencheck: Ökobilanz von Suchmaschinen. *SWR 04* (09): 2018. https://www.swr.de/wissen/20-%20jahre-google-umwelt-facts-zu-suchmaschinen//id=253126/did=22378814/%20nid=253126/d2azhl/index.html.

Eckoldt, Matthias. 2018. Das Fenster zum Hirn, *Deutschlandfunk* (Ursendung: 16.08.2018). https://www.deutschlandfunkkultur.de/gedankenlesen-mit-neurowissenschaft-das-fenster-zum-hirn.976.de.html?dram:article_id=425645.

Ekman, Ulrik. 2016. Introduction. Complex ubiquity-effects. In *Ubiquitous computing, complexity and Culture*, ed. Ulrik Ekman, Jay David Bolter, Lily Díaz, Morten Søndergaard, and Maria Engberg, 39–74. New York: Routledge.

Emerson, Lori. 2014. *Reading writing interfaces: From the digital to the bookbound*. Minneapolis: University of Minnesota Press.

References

Engemann, Christoph. 2018. Rekursionen über Körper. Machine Learning-Trainingsdatensätze als Arbeit am Index. In *Machine learning. Medien, Infrastrukturen und Technologien der Künstlichen Intelligenz*, ed. Christoph Engemann and Andreas Sudmann, 247–268. Bielefeld: transcript.

Ernst, Christoph and Jens Schröter, eds. 2017. *Navigationen–Zeitschrift für Medien- und Kulturwissenschaften* 17:2 (Medien, Interfaces und implizites Wissen). Siegen: universi.

Europäische Kommission (EK). 2018a. *Mitteilung der Kommission an das Europäische Parlament, den Rat, den Europäischen Wirtschafts- und Sozialausschuss und den Ausschuss der Regionen*. Bekämpfung von Desinformation im Internet–ein europäisches Konzept. https://eur-lex.europa.eu/legal-content/DE/TXT/PDF/?uri=CELEX:52018DC0236&from=DE.

———. 2018b. *Mitteilung der Kommission an das Europäische Parlament, den Rat, den Europäischen Wirtschafts- und Sozialausschuss und den Ausschuss der Regionen: Koordinierter Plan für künstliche Intelligenz*. https://ec.europa.eu/transparency/regdoc/rep/1/2018/DE/COM-2018-795-F1-DE-MAIN-PART-1.PDF.

Farocki, Harun. 2004. Quereinfluss / Weiche Montage. In: *Zeitsprünge. Wie Filme Geschichte(n) erzählen*, ed. Christine Rüffert et al., 57–61. Berlin: Bertz.

FDP-Bundesgeschäftsstelle (FDP). 2017. *Kampagnenkatalog Bundestagswahl 2017*. Berlin: FDP.

Föderl-Schmid, Alexandra and Simon Hurz: Wie Überwachung gegen das Virus helfen könnte. Süddeutsche Zeitung, 23.03.2020. https://sz.de/1.4855065.

Foucault, Michel, and Didier Eribon. 2005. Ist es also wichtig zu denken? In *Dits et Ecrits. Schriften, Bd. IV, 1980–1988*, ed. Michel Foucault, 219–223. Frankfurt a. M, Suhrkamp.

Foucault, Michel. 1980. The confession of the flesh. In *Power/knowledge. Selected interviews and other writings 1972–1977*, ed. Colin Gordon, 194–228. New York: Pantheon Books.

———. 1987. Das Subjekt und die Macht. In *Michel Foucault. Jenseits von Strukturalismus und Hermeneutik*, ed. Hubert L. Dreyfus and Paul Rabinow, 243–261. Frankfurt a. M: Athenäum.

———. 1982. The subject and power. *Critical Inquiry* 8 (4): 777–795.

Franke, Anselm, Stephanie Hankey, and Marek Tuszynski, eds. 2016. *Nervous systems. Quantified life and the social question*. Berlin: Spector.

Franklin, Seb. 2015. *Control: Digitality as cultural logic*. Cambridge: MIT Press.

Friedrich, Kathrin. 2021. Im virtuellen Zaun. Umgebungen adaptiver Medien. In *Techno-ästhetische Perspektivierungen des Milieus. Ein Reader*, ed. Rebekka Ladewig and Angelika Seppi. Leipzig: Spector Books.

Gabrys, Jennifer. 2014. Programming environments. Environmentality and citizen sensing in the Smart City. *Environment and Planning D: Society and Space* 32: 30–48.

———. 2016. *Program earth: Environmental sensing technology and the making of a computational planet.* Minneapolis: University of Minnesota Press.

———. 2019. Sensors and sensing practices: Reworking experience across entities, environments, and technologies. *Science, Technology, & Human Values* 44 (5): 723–736.

Gallagher, Ryan, and Ludovica Jona. 2019. We tested Europe's new lie detector for travelers–and immediately triggered a false positive. *The Intercept* 26 (07): 2019. https://theintercept.com/2019/07/26/europe-border-control-ai-lie-detector/.

Galloway, Alexander R. 2004. *Protocol: How control exists after decentralization.* Cambridge: MIT Press.

———. 2006. Language wants to be overlooked: On software and ideology. *Journal of Visual Culture* 5: 315–331.

———. 2011. Black box, black bloc. In *Communization and its discontents: Contestation, critique, and contemporary struggles*, ed. Benjamin Noys, 237–252. New York: Autonomedia.

———. 2012. *The Interface effect.* Cambridge: Polity Press.

———. 2014. *Laruelle: Against the digital.* Minneapolis: University of Minnesota Press.

Galloway, Alexander R., and Martina Leeker. 2017. Intervening infrastructures: Ad hoc networking and liberated computer language. In *Interventions in digital cultures: Technology, the political, methods*, ed. Howard Caygill, Martina Leeker, and Tobias Schulze, 61–72. Lüneburg: Meson Press.

Garcés, Marina. 2008. What Are We Capable Of? From Consciousness to Embodiment in Critical Thought Today. *transversal* 4. https://transversal.at/transversal/0808/garces/en.

Gerling, Winfried, Susanne Holschbach, and Petra Löffler. 2018. *Bilder verteilen. Fotografische Praktiken in der digitalen Kultur.* Bielefeld: transcript.

Gerlitz, Carolin, Anne Helmond, David B. Nieborg and Fernando N. van der Vlist. 2019. Apps and infrastructures–A research agenda. *Computational Culture* 7. https://computationalculture.net/apps-and-infrastructures-a-research-agenda/.

Gerlitz, Carolin, and Anne Helmond. 2013. The like economy: Social buttons and the data-intensive web. *New Media & Society* 15 (8): 1348–1365.

Gethmann, Daniel, and Florian Sprenger. 2014. *Die Enden des Kabels. Kleine Mediengeschichte der Übertragung.* Berlin: Kadmos.

Gießmann, Sebastian, and Marcus Burkhardt. 2014. Was ist Datenkritik? Zur Einführung. *Mediale Kontrolle unter Beobachtung* 3 (1) www.medialekontrolle.de/ausgaben/3-12014-datenkritik.

Gray, George W. 1925. The bottom of the ocean is ‚Main Street' to him. The American Magazine 99 (1): 48–49., 130–132.
Gresser, Uwe. 2018. *Praxishandbuch Hochfrequenzhandel (Band 2)–Advanced: Produkte, Systeme, Regulierung*. Wiesbaden: Springer Gabler.
Grimm, Jacob and Wilhelm Grimm. 1873. *Deutsches Wörterbuch* (16 Bde. in 32 Teilbänden, Leipzig 1854–1961, Bd. 11 [1873], Sp. 2336, Lemma "Kritik"). https://www.woerterbuchnetz.de/DWB?lemma=kritik.
———. 1885. *Deutsches Wörterbuch* (16 Bde. in 32 Teilbänden, Leipzig 1854–1961, Bd. 12 [1885], Spalte 728–733, Lemma "Leiten"). https://www.woerterbuchnetz.de/DWB?lemma=leiten.
Grosser, Benjamin. 2014. What do metrics want? How quantification prescribes social interaction on Facebook. *Computational Culture* 4. https://computationalculture.net/what-do-metrics-want/.
———. 2018. Facebook Demetricator. https://vimeo.com/249448543.
Hadler, Florian, and Joachim Haupt, eds. 2016. *Interface Critique*. Berlin: Kadmos.
Hadler, Florian, Alice Soiné, and Daniel Irrgang, eds. 2018. *Interface Critique Journal* 1.
——— eds. 2019. *Interface Critique Journal* 2.
Hagen, Wolfgang. 2018. Anästhetische Ästhetiken. Über Smartphone-Bilder und ihre Ökologie. In *Smartphone-Ästhetik. Zur Philosophie und Gestaltung mobiler Medien*, ed. Oliver Ruf, 75–104. Bielefeld: transcript.
Hansen, Mark B.N. 2013. Ubiquitous sensation: Towards an atmospheric, impersonal and mircotemporal media. In *Throughout. Art and Culture emerging with ubiquitous computing*, ed. Ulrik Ekman, 63–88. Cambridge: MIT Press.
———. 2015. *Feed forward. On the future of twenty-first-century-media*. Chicago: University of Chicago Press.
Hartmann, Frank. 2014. Mediologie. *Handbuch Medienwissenschaft*, ed. Jens Schröter. Stuttgart/Weimar: Metzler, 159–165.
Hassan, Robert. 2020. *The condition of digitality: A post-modern marxism for the practice of digital life*. London: University of Westminster Press.
Hayles, Katherine N. 2016. Foreword. In *Ubiquitous computing, complexity and Culture*, ed. Ulrik Ekman, Jay David Bolter, Lily Díaz, Morten Søndergaard, and Maria Engberg, 33–38. New York: Routledge.
Hayward, Susan. 2013. *Cinema studies. The key concepts*. New York: Routledge.
Heilmann, Till A. 2015. Datenarbeit im 'Capture'-Kapitalismus. Zur Ausweitung der Verwertungszone im Zeitalter informatischer Überwachung. *Zeitschrift für Medienwissenschaft* 13: 35–47.
———. 2018. Es gibt keine Software. Noch immer nicht oder nicht mehr. In *Smartphone-Ästhetik. Zur Philosophie und Gestaltung mobiler Medien*, ed. Oliver Ruf, 159–179. Bielefeld: transcript.
Hellige, Hans Dieter. 2008. Krisen- und Innovationsphasen in der Mensch-Computer-Interaktion. In *Mensch-Computer-Interface. Zur Geschichte*

und Zukunft der Computerbedienung, ed. Hans Dieter Hellige, 11–92. Bielefeld: transcript.

Holert, Tom. 2002. Globodigitalizität. *Über die Zumutung des Evidenten.* www.khm.de/kmw/kit/pdf/holert.pdf.

Hookway, Branden. 2014. *Interfaces*. Cambridge: MIT Press.

Hörl, Erich. 2008. Die offene Maschine. Heidegger, Günther und Simondon über die technologische Bedingung. *MLN* 123 (3): 632–655.

———. 2016. Die Ökologisierung des Denkens. *Zeitschrift für Medienwissenschaft* 14: 33–45.

———. 2018. Die environmentalitäre Situation. Überlegungen zum Umweltlich-Werden von Denken, Macht und Kapital. *Internationales Jahrbuch für Medienphilosophie* 4: 221–250.

Hörl, Erich, Nelly Y. Pinkrah, and Lotte Warnsholdt, eds. 2021. *Critique and the digital*. Zürich: Diaphanes.

Hu, Tung-Hui. 2015. *A prehistory of the cloud*. Cambridge: MIT Press.

Hui, Yuk. 2015. Induction, deduction and transduction: On the aesthetics and logic of digital objects. *Networking Knowledge* 8 (3): 1–19. https://doi.org/10.31165/nk.2015.83.376.

———. 2016a. *On the existence of digital objects*. Minneapolis: University of Minnesota Press.

———. 2016b. *The question concerning technology in China. An essay in cosmotechnics*. Falmouth: Urbanomic Media.

iBorderCtrl. 2016a. *Technical Framework*.https://perma.cc/9MKY-GAFC.

———. 2016b. *Intelligent portable control system*.https://ec.europa.eu/research/participants/documents/downloadPublic?documentIds=080166e5cc60c9b0&appId=PPGMS.

Jeong, Seung-hoon. 2013. *Cinematic interfaces: Film theory after new media*. New York: Routledge.

Jin, Dal Yong. 2015. *Digital platforms, imperialism and political Culture*. New York: Routledge.

Kaerlein, Timo. 2018. *Smartphones als digitale Nahkörpertechnologien. Zur Kybernetisierung des Alltags*. Bielefeld: transcript.

———. 2020. Interface. Zur Vermittlung von Praktiken und Infrastrukturen (als Perspektive für die Medienwissenschaft). In *Wovon sprechen wir, wenn wir von Digitalisierung sprechen?* In *Gehalte und Revisionen zentraler Begriffe des Digitalen*, ed. Martin Huber, Sybille Krämer, and Claus Pias, 45–58. Frankfurt am Main: CompaRe.

Kaldrack, Irina, and Martina Leeker. 2015. Introduction. In *There is no software, there are just services*, ed. Irina Kaldrack and Martina Leeker, 9–20. Lüneburg: Meson Press.

Kay, Alan C. 2001. User interface–a personal view (1989). In *Multimedia. From Wagner to virtual reality*, ed. Randall Packer and Ken Jordan, 121–131. New York: Norton.

Kierkegaard, Søren. 1983. *The sickness unto death*. Princeton: Princeton University Press.

References

Kim, Changwook. 2018. Digitalization, labor flexibility and the change of cultural production in the Korean broadcasting industry. In *Digital Korea: Digital technology and the change of social life*, ed. Wooyeol Shin Kyunghee Kim and Changwook Kim, 163–185. Seoul: Hanul.

King, Homay, and Regina Longo. 2015. The digital, the virtual, and the possible. Riffing with Homay King on virtual memory: Time-based media art and the dream of Digitality. *Film Quarterly* 69 (1): 93–96.

Kittler, Friedrich. 1986. *Grammophon, film, typewriter*. Berlin: Brinkmann & Bose.

Kittler, Friedrich. 1993. Es gibt keine Software. In *Draculas Vermächtnis. Technische Schriften*, ed. Friedrich Kittler, 225–243. Leipzig: Reclam.

———. 1994a. Protected Mode. In *Computer als Medium*, ed. Norbert Bolz, Friedrich Kittler, and Christoph Tholen, 209–220. München: Fink.

———. 1994b. Wenn die Freiheit wirklich existiert, dann soll sie doch ausbrechen. In *Am Ende vorbei*, ed. Rudolf Maresch, 95–129. Wien: Turia & Kant.

———. 2008. Code (or, how you can write something differently). In *Software studies: A lexicon*, ed. Matthew Fuller, 40–47. Cambridge: MIT Press.

Knop, Carsten. 2018. Facebook ist von innen faul. *Frankfurter Allgemeine Zeitung*. https://www.faz.net/-ikh-9hug1.

Krajewski, Markus. 2019. Hilfe für die Hilfswissenschaft. *Frankfurter Allgemeine Zeitung*, N4.

Krämer, Sybille. 2003. 'Schriftbildlichkeit' oder: Über eine (fast) vergessene Dimension der Schrift. In *Bild, Schrift, Zahl*, ed. Sybille Krämer and Horst Bredekamp, 157–176. Paderborn: Fink.

———. 2018. Der 'Stachel des Digitalen'–ein Anreiz zur Selbstreflexion in den Geisteswissenschaften? Ein philosophischer Kommentar zu den Digital Humanities in neun Thesen. *Digital Classics Online* 4 (1): 37–43.

———. 2019. Algorithmen als Erben des Alphabets? Über die "neue Intransparenz" und das Projekt "digitaler Aufklärung". In *Das Neue alphabet. Opening days*, ed. Bernd Scherer and Olga von Schubert, 53–56. Berlin: HKW.

Krishnan, Aishwarya, and Anirban Hal. 2018. The perfect enterprise device to watch out for–Huawei mate. *Gadgets Now* 04 (12): 2020. https://www.gadgetsnow.com/gn-advertorial/the-perfect-enterprise-device-to-watch-out-for-huawei-mate-20-pro/articleshow/66936825.cms.

Kümmel, Albert. 2004. Ferne Bilder, so nah (Deutschland 1926). In *Analog/Digital–Opposition oder Kontinuum? Zur Theorie und Geschichte einer Unterscheidung*, ed. Jens Schröter and Alexander Böhnke, 279–294. Bielefeld: transcript.

Küpper, Moritz. 2022. Interview Volker Wissing zu G7-Digitalministertreffen. *Deutschlandfunk* (Ursendung: 10.05.2022). https://www.deutschlandfunk.de/interview-volker-wissing-bundesminister-zu-g7-digitalministertreffen-dlf-0e612531-100.html.

Lahiri Choudhury, Deep Kanta. 2010. *Telegraphic imperialism: Crisis and panic in the Indian empire, c.1830–1920*. Basingstoke: Palgrave Macmillan.

Lapuschkin, Sebastian, et al. 2019. Unmasking clever Hans predictors and assessing what machines really learn. *Nature Communications* 10 (1): 1–8. https://doi.org/10.1038/s41467-019-08987-4.

Lanier, Jaron. 2018. *Ten arguments for deleting your social media accounts right now*. New York: Henry Holt.

Latour, Bruno. 1993. *We have never been modern*. Cambridge: Harvard University Press.

———. 2004. Why has critique run out of steam? From matters of fact to matters of concern. *Critical Inquiry* 30 (2): 225–248.

———. 2011. Networks, societies, spheres: Reflections of an actor-network theorist international. *Journal of Communication* 5: 796–810.

Lazzarato, Maurizio. 1998. Immaterielle Arbeit. Gesellschaftliche Tätigkeit unter den Bedingungen des Postfordismus. In *Umherschweifende Produzenten. Immaterielle Arbeit und Subversion*, ed. Antonio Negri, Maurizio Lazzarato, and Paolo Virno, 39–52. Berlin: ID-Verlag.

Li, Yueqing, and Chang S. Nam. 2016. A collaborative brain-computer interface (BCI) for ALS patients. *Proceedings of the Human Factors and Ergonomics Society Annual Meeting* 59 (1): 716–720.

Light, Ben, Jean Burgess, and Stefanie Duguay. 2018. The walkthrough method: An approach to the study of apps. *New Media & Society*, 20 (3): 881–890.

Lovelace, Ada. 1842. Note A. Sketch of The Analytical Engine Invented by Charles Babbage, from the Bibliothèque Universelle de Genève October 1842 No. 82 with notes upon the Memoir by the Translator Ada Augusta Countess of Lovelace, edit. L. F. Menabrea and Ada Lovelace, www.fourmilab.ch/babbage/sketch.html.

Lovink, Geert. 2012. *Networks without a cause. A critique of social media*. Cambridge: Polity.

———. 2016. *Social media abyss. Critical internet cultures and the force of negation*. Cambridge: Polity.

Lund, Holger. 2017. What's left? The critique of digital life in hyper-digital music videos. In *Daniel Kulle*, ed. Post-Digital Culture. Oliver Schmidt and David Ziegenhagen: Cornelia Lund. https://www.post-digital-culture.org/hlund2.

Lutz, Jens, Miriam Stürner, Daria Mille, and Giulia Bini, eds. 2015. *Infosphäre*. Karlsruhe: ZKM.

Mandl, Peter. 2010. *Grundkurs Betriebssysteme. Architekturen, Betriebsmittelverwaltung, Synchronisation, Prozesskommunikation*. Wiesbaden: GWV.

Manovich, Lev. 2001. *The language of new media*. Cambridge: MIT Press.

Mantz, Jeffrey W. 2008. Blood diamonds of the digital age: Coltan and the eastern Congo. *Global Studies Review* 4 (3): 12–14.

References

Maresch, Rudolf and Florian Rötzer, eds. 2001. *Cyberhypes. Möglichkeiten und Grenzen des Internet*. Frankfurt a. M.: Suhrkamp.

Maresch, Rudolf. 2004. Virtualität. In *Glossar der Gegenwart*, ed. Ulrich Bröckling, Susanne Krasmann and Thomas Lemke, 277–284. Frankfurt a. M.: Suhrkamp.

Marks, Laura U. 2020. *Streaming video, a link between pandemic and climate crisis*. *Rosa Mercedes* 2: https://www.harun-farocki-institut.org/en/2020/04/16/streaming-video-a-link-between-pandemic-and-climate-crisis-journal-of-visual-culture-hafi-2/.

Marx, Paris. 2020. Nationalize Amazon. *Jacobin* 29 (03): 2020. https://www.jacobinmag.com/2020/03/nationalize-amazon-coronavirus-delivery-usps.

Maschewski, Felix, and Anna Verena Nosthoff. 2019. Netzwerkaffekte. Über Facebook als kybernetische Regierungsmaschine und das Verschwinden des Subjekts. In *Affekt Macht Netz. Auf dem Weg zu einer Sozialtheorie der Digitalen Gesellschaft*, ed. Anja Breljak, Rainer Mühlhoff, and Jan Slaby, 55–80. Bielefeld: transcript.

Mayer, Michael. 2018. Die Diskretion des Digitalen (Kapital als Medium II). *Internationales Jahrbuch für Medienphilosophie* 4: 25–53.

Mbembe, Achille. 2015. The internet is afropolitan. In *#game changer. How is new media changing political participation in Africa?* ed. Keren Ben-Zeev and Jochen Luckscheiter, 30–35. Cape Town: Heinrich-Böll-Stiftung.

———. 2017. *Critique of black reason*. Durham: Duke University Press.

Mersch, Dieter. 1991. Digitalität und Nicht-Diskursives Denken. In *Computer, Kultur, geschichte. Beiträge zu einer Philosophie des Informationszeitalters*, ed. Dieter Mersch and Kristóf Nyíri, 109–126. Wien: Passagen.

———. 2016. Kritik der Operativität. Bemerkungen zu einem technologischen Imperativ. *Internationales Jahrbuch für Medienphilosophie* 2: 25–53.

———. 2017. Digital Criticism. Für eine Kritik, 'algorithmischer' Vernunft. *Diaphanes Magazin* 3. https://www.diaphanes.net/titel/digital-criticism-5312.

———. 2019. Kreativität und Künstliche Intelligenz. Einige Bemerkungen zu einer Kritik algorithmischer Rationalität. *Zeitschrift für Medienwissenschaft* 21: 65–74.

Meyer, Jens-Uwe. 2020. Wie Corona die Arbeitswelt langfristig verändert. *Manager Magazin* 20 (03): 2020. https://www.manager-magazin.de/unternehmen/artikel/durchbruch-fuer-digitalisierung-corona-veraendert-die-arbeitswelt-a-1305535.html.

Mirowski, Philip. 2002. *Machine dreams. Economics becomes a cyborg science*. New York: Cambridge University Press.

Moll, Joana. 2018. Research Values: Deep Carbon. https://researchvalues2018.wordpress.com/2018/01/03/joana-moll-deep-carbon/.

———. 2022. Joana Moll. https://www.janavirgin.com/index.html.

Morozov, Evgeny. 2013. Der Preis der Heuchelei. *Frankfurter Allgemeine Zeitung*, 25.

———. 2019. Vom digitalen Widerstand. *Süddeutsche Zeitung*, 17.

Mühlhoff, Rainer. 2019. Menschengestützte künstliche Intelligenz. Über die soziotechnischen Voraussetzungen von "deep learning". *Zeitschrift für Medienwissenschaft* 21: 56–64.

Müller, Daniel, and Annemone Ligensa. 2009. Einleitung. In *Leitmedien. Konzepte–Relevanz–geschichte*, ed. Daniel Müller, Annemone Ligensa, and Peter Gendolla, 11–27. Bielefeld: transcript.

Müller, Martin U. 2020. Doktor auf Distanz. *Der Spiegel* 15: 76–77.

Murali, Vijayaraghavan et al. 2018. Neural sketch learning for conditional program generation. Conference paper at International Conference on Learning Representations (ICLR) 2018. https://arxiv.org/pdf/1703.05698.pdf.

Musk, Elon, and Neuralink. 2019. An integrated brain-machine Interface platform with thousands of channels. *Journal of Medical Internet Research* 21 (10): 10.2196/16194.

Mussler, Werner. 2017. Der Weg zur Internet-Steuer in Europa ist weit. *Frankfurter Allgemeine Zeitung* 21 (09): 2017. https://www.faz.net/-gqi-9200t.

Nake, Frieder. 2021/1984. Schnittstelle Mensch-Maschine. In *Algorithmen & Zeichen. Beiträge von Frieder Nake zur Gegenwart des Computers*, ed. Jan Distelmeyer, Sophie Ehrmanntraut, and Boris Müller, 274–286. Berlin: Kadmos.

———. 2021/1986. Die Verdoppelung des Werkzeugs. In *Algorithmen & Zeichen. Beiträge von Frieder Nake zur Gegenwart des Computers*, ed. Jan Distelmeyer, Sophie Ehrmanntraut, and Boris Müller, 288–301. Berlin: Kadmos.

———. 2021/2001.Vilém Flusser und Max Bense des Pixels angesichtig werdend. Eine Überlegung am Rande der Computergrafik. In *Algorithmen & Zeichen. Beiträge von Frieder Nake zur Gegenwart des Computers*, ed. Jan Distelmeyer, Sophie Ehrmanntraut, and Boris Müller, 22–35. Berlin: Kadmos.

———. 2021/2003. Subjekt & Objekt. Participatory design/object oriented design. Eine Reflexion. In *Algorithmen & Zeichen. Beiträge von Frieder Nake zur Gegenwart des Computers*, ed. Jan Distelmeyer, Sophie Ehrmanntraut, and Boris Müller, 302–316. Berlin: Kadmos.

———. 2021/2009. Pinsel, Bleistift, Schere, Lasso und der ganze Werkzeugkasten. Instrument als Medium. In *Algorithmen & Zeichen. Beiträge von Frieder Nake zur Gegenwart des Computers*, ed. Jan Distelmeyer, Sophie Ehrmanntraut, and Boris Müller, 318–337. Berlin: Kadmos.

———. 2021/2016. The disappearing masterpiece. Digital image & algorithmic revolution. In *Algorithmen & Zeichen. Beiträge von Frieder Nake zur Gegenwart des Computers*, ed. Jan Distelmeyer, Sophie Ehrmanntraut, and Boris Müller, 122–147. Berlin: Kadmos.

References

Negroponte, Nicholas. 1995a. *Being digital*. New York: Alfred A. Knopf.

———. 1995b. *Total digital. Die Welt zwischen 0 und 1 oder Die Zukunft der Kommunikation*. München: Bertelsmann.

Neuralink. 2020. *Watch Live! Elon Musk's neuralink demonstrates its brain to machine interface*. https://www.youtube.com/watch?v=Mp6_ZHHGIF8&t=2s.

Nikl, Wilhelm Possidius. 1866. *Blicke in die Etymologie der deutschen Sprache: ein Beitrag zum Verständniß derselben für Studierende*. Neuburg: Rindfleisch.

Noble, Safiya Umoja. 2018. *Algorithms of oppression: How search engines reinforce racism*. New York: New York University Press.

Nohr, Rolf F. 2014. *Nützliche Bilder. Bild, Diskurs, Evidenz*. Münster: Lit.

O'Shea, James. 2018. Intelligent deception detection through machine. *IJCNN* 1–8. https://doi.org/10.1109/IJCNN.2018.8489392.

Obama, Barack. 2009. *Public papers of the presidents of the United States: Barack Obama (2009, book I)*. Washington: U.S. Government Printing Office.

Ochsner, Beate. 2016. Der Begriff des Digitalen: Das Wort der Stunde. *Frankfurter Allgemeine Zeitung* 22 (02): 2016. https://www.faz.net/-gsf-8dvug.

Oberndörfer, Mathias. 2018. Digitale Konvergenz ist essenziell für Deutschlands Wohlstand. *Die Welt*. 21 (08): 2018. https://www.welt.de/wirtschaft/bilanz/article181248698/.

Ohlberg, Mareike. 2019. Digitaler big brother. *Internationale Politik* 2: 60–67.

Parisi, Luciana. 2017. Computational logic and ecological rationality. In *General ecology: The new ecological paradigm*, ed. Erich Hörl and James Burton, 75–100. London: Bloomsbury.

———. 2018. Das Lernen lernen oder die algorithmische Entdeckung von Informationen. In *Machine learning. Medien, Infrastrukturen und Technologien der Künstlichen Intelligenz*, ed. Christoph Engemann and Andreas Sudmann, 93–113. Bielefeld: transcript.

———. 2019. The alien subject of AI. *Subjectivity* 12: 27–48.

Parisi, Luciana, and Erich Hörl. 2013. Was heißt Medienästhetik? Ein Gespräch über algorithmische Ästhetik, automatisches Denken und die postkybernetische Logik der Komputation. *Zeitschrift für Medienwissenschaft* 8: 35–51.

Parikka, Jussi. 2015. *A geology of media*. Minneapolis: University of Minnesota Press.

Parks, Lisa, and Nicole Starosielski. 2015. Introduction. In *Signal traffic: Critical studies of media infrastructures*, ed. Lisa Parls and Nicole Starosielski, 1–27. Illinois: University of Illinois Press.

Pasquinelli, Matteo. 2019. 3000 Years of algorithmic rituals: The emergence of AI from the computation of space. *e-flux Journal* 101. https://www.e-flux.com/journal/101/273221/three-thousand-years-of-algorithmic-rituals-the-emergence-of-ai-from-the-computation-of-space/.

Paul, Christiane. 2007. The myth of immateriality: Presenting and preserving new media. In *MediaArtHistories*, ed. Oliver Grau, 251–274. Cambridge: MIT Press.

Peirce, Charles Sanders. 1998. What is a sign. In *The essential Peirce: Selected philosophical writings (1893–1913)*, ed. The Peirce Edition Project, 4–10. Bloomington: Indiana University Press.

Perricos, Costi, and Vishal Kapur. 2019. Anticipatory government. Preempting problems through predictive analytics. In *Deloitte Insights: Government Trends 2020*, ed. William Eggers, 41–47. https://www2.deloitte.com/content/dam/insights/us/articles/government-trends-2020/DI_Government-Trends-2020.pdf.

Pias, Claus. 2000. *Computer Spiel Welten*. Weimar: Universität Weimar. ftp://ftp.uni-weimar.de/pub/publications/diss/Pias/pias.pdf.

———. 2004. Zeit der Kybernetik–Eine Einstimmung. In *Cybernetics–Kybernetik. The Macy-conferences 1946–1953 (volume II)*, ed. Claus Pias, 9–41. Zürich/Berlin: Diaphanes.

Pourghomi, Pardis, et al. 2017. *How to stop spread of misinformation on social media: Facebook plans vs. right-click authenticate approach.* ICEMIS: 1–18. https://doi.org/10.1109/ICEMIS.2017.8272957.

Qiu, Jack Linchuan, and Yeran Kim. 2010. Recession and progression? Notes on media, labor, and youth from East Asia international. *Journal of Communication* 4: 630–648.

Qiu, Jack Linchuan. 2012. Network labor. Beyond the shadow of Foxconn. In *Studying mobile media. Cultural technologies, mobile communication, and the iPhone*, ed. Larissa Hjorth, Jean Burgess, and Ingrid Richardson, 173–189. New York: Routledge.

Rahawan, Iyad. 2019. Unwissen macht uns manipulierbar. *Der Spiegel* 25: 102–104.

Reckwitz, Andreas. 2018. *Die Gesellschaft der Singularitäten: Zum Strukturwandel der Moderne*. Frankfurt a. M: Suhrkamp.

Reichert, Ramón. 2009. *Das Wissen der Börse: Medien und Praktiken des Finanzmarktes*. Bielefeld: transcript.

Renn, Jürgen, and Bernd Scherer, eds. 2015. *Das Anthropozän. Ein Zwischenbericht*. Berlin: Matthes & Seitz.

Ribeiro, Fabíola M., and Rejane Spitz. 2006. Archigram's analogical approach to digitality. *International Journal of Architectural Computing* 4 (3): 19–32.

Ring, Uli. 2009. *Substantivderivation in der Urkundensprache des 13. Jahrhunderts. Eine historisch-synchrone Untersuchung anhand der ältesten deutschsprachigen Originalurkunden (Studia Linguistica Germanica, Band 96)*. Berlin/New York: De Gruyter.

Ripley, M. Louise. 2008. Trickster fiddles with informatics: The social impact of technological marketing schemes. *Journal of Systemics, Cybernetics, and Informatics* 6 (1): 91–96.

Ritzer, Ivo. 2018. *Medientheorie der Globalisierung*. Wiesbaden: Springer VS.

Robert Koch-Institut (RKI). 2020a. Corona-Datenspende-App. https://www.rki.de/DE/Content/InfAZ/N/Neuartiges_Coronavirus/Corona-Datenspende-allgemein.html.

———. 2020b. Grafiken zur App "Corona-Datenspende". https://www.rki.de/DE/Content/Service/Presse/Pressefotos/Corona-Datenspende.html.

Robben, Bernard, and Heidi Schelhowe. 2012. Was heißt be-greifbare Interaktion? In *Be-greifbare Interaktionen. Der allgegenwärtige Computer: Touchscreens, wearables, tangibles und ubiquitous computing*, ed. Bernard Robben and Heidi Schelhowe, 7–15. Bielefeld: transcript.

Robben, Bernard. 2012. Die Bedeutung der Körperlichkeit für begreifbare Interaktion mit dem Computer. In *Be-greifbare Interaktionen. Der allgegenwärtige Computer: Touchscreens, wearables, tangibles und ubiquitous computing*, ed. Bernard Robben and Heidi Schelhowe, 19–39. Bielefeld: transcript.

Rose, Gillian. 2014. Networks, interfaces, and computer-generated images: Learning from digital visualisations of urban redevelopment projects. *Environment and Planning D: Society and Space* 32 (3): 386–403.

Roose, Kevin. 2020. The coronavirus crisis is showing us how to live online. *The New York Times* 17 (03): 2020. https://nyti.ms/2vx0xn0.

Rosenfeld, Dagmar. 2020. Das Digitale hält uns jetzt zusammen. *Die Welt* 17 (03): 2020. https://www.welt.de/debatte/kommentare/article206619163/Corona-Krise-Das-Digitale-haelt-uns-jetzt-zusammen.html.

Röttgers, Kurt. 1975. *Kritik und Praxis. Zur geschichte des Kritikbegriffs von Kant bis Marx*. Berlin/New York: De Gruyter.

Rötzer, Florian. 1991. *Digitaler Schein. Ästhetik der elektronischen Medien*. Frankfurt a. M: Suhrkamp.

Rouvroy, Antoinette. 2013. The end(s) of critique. Data behaviourism versus due process. In *Privacy, due process and the computational turn*, ed. Mireille Hildebrandt and Katja de Vries, 142–168. London: Routledge.

Rouvroy, Antoinette, and Thomas Berns. 2013. Algorithmic governmentality and prospects of emancipation: Disparateness as a precondition for individuation through relationships? *Réseaux* 177: 163–196.

Schaefer, Peter. 2011. Interface: History of a concept, 1868–1888. In *The long history of new media: Technology, historiography, and contextualizing newness*, ed. David W. Park, Nicholas W. Jankowski, and Steve Jones, 163–117. New York: Lang.

Schäfer, Jörgen. 2004. Sprachzeichenprozesse. Überlegungen zur Codierung von Literatur in 'alten' und 'neuen' Medien. In *Analog/Digital–Opposition oder Kontinuum? Zur Theorie und Geschichte einer Unterscheidung*, ed. Jens Schröter and Alexander Böhnke, 143–168. Bielefeld: transcript.

Scharre, Paul. 2018. *Army of none: Autonomous weapons and the future of war*. New York: Norton.

Scheffler, Hermann. 1877. *Die Naturgesetze und ihr Zusammenhang mit den abstrakten Wissenschaften. Zweiter Teil: Die Theorie der Erscheinung oder die physischen Gesetze*. Leipzig: Friedrich Foerster.

Schmidt, Martin. 2015. Kanalisieren. In *Historisches Wörterbuch des Mediengebrauchs*, ed. Heiko Christians, Matthias Bickenbach, and Nikolaus Wegmann, 322–331. Köln: Böhlau.

Schneider, Birgit. 2019. Mensch-Maschine-Schnittstellen in Technosphäre und Anthropozän. In *Mensch-Maschine-Interaktion. Handbuch zur Geschichte, Kultur, Ethik*, ed. Kevin Liggieri and Oliver Müller, 95–105. Stuttgart: Metzler.

———. 2020. Funknetze und ihre Tarnungen als Technohabitate für Menschen, Pflanzen, Tiere und Maschinen. In *Milieu Fragmente. Technologische und ästhetische Perspektive*, ed. Rebekka Ladewig and Angelika Seppi, 356–368. Leipzig: Spector Books.

Schröter, Jens. 2004. In *Analog/Digital–Opposition oder Kontinuum? In Analog/Digital–Opposition oder Kontinuum? Zur Theorie und Geschichte einer Unterscheidung*, ed. Jens Schröter and Alexander Böhnke, 7–30. Bielefeld: transcript.

———. 2016. Digitalität und die Medienwissenschaft. *Digitalität. Theorien und Praktiken des Digitalen in den Geisteswissenschaften*. https://digigeist.hypotheses.org/86#more-86.

Schröter, Jens, and Till A. Heilmann. 2016. Statt einer Einleitung: Zum Bonner Programm einer neo-kritischen Medienwissenschaft. In *Navigationen–Zeitschrift für Medien- und Kulturwissenschaften 16:2 (Medienwissenschaft und Kapitalismuskritik)*, ed. Jens Schröter and Till A. Heilmann, 7–36. Siegen: universi.

Schulz, Martin. 2015. Vorwort. In *Technologischer Totalitarismus. Eine Debatte*, ed. Frank Schirrmacher, 9–13. Frankfurt a. M: Suhrkamp.

Selfe, Cynthia L., and Richard J. Selfe. 1994. The politics of the interface: Power and its exercise in electronic contact zones. *National Council of Teachers of English* 45 (4): 480–504.

Smith, Crosbie, and M. Norton Wise. 1989. *Energy and empire: A biographical study of Lord Kelvin*. Cambridge: MIT Press.

Smith, Karl U. 1963. Computer systems control of delayed auditory feedback. *Perceptual and Motor Skills* 17: 343–354.

Snickars, Pelle. 2012. A walled garden turned into a rain forest. In *Moving data. The iPhone and the future of media*, ed. Pelle Snickars and Patrick Vonderau, 155–168. New York: Columbia University Press.

Sprenger, Florian. 2015. *Politik der Mikroentscheidungen*. Lüneburg: Meson Press.

Sprenger, Florian, and Christoph Engemann. 2015. *Internet der Dinge. Über smarte Objekte, intelligente Umgebungen und die technische Durchdringung der welt*. Bielefeld: transcript.

Srinivasan, Sharath, Stephanie Diepeveen, and George Karekwaivanane. 2019. Rethinking publics in Africa in a digital age. *Journal of Eastern African Studies* 13 (1): 2–17.

Srnicek, Nick. 2017. *Platform capitalism*. Cambridge: Polity Press.

Staab, Philipp. 2019. *Digitaler Kapitalismus. Markt und Herrschaft in der Ökonomie der Unknappheit*. Berlin: Suhrkamp.

Stalder, Felix. 2016. *Kultur der Digitalität*. Berlin: Suhrkamp.

Stalder, Felix. 2017. *The digital condition*. Cambridge: Polity Press.

Starosielski, Nicole. 2015. *The undersea network*. Durham: Duke University Press.

Statista Research Department, Global smartphone penetration, https://www.statista.com/statistics/203734/global-smartphone-penetration-per-capita-since-2005/ (2022).

Stiftungsverband Rat für Kulturelle Bildung (RatKuBi). 2019. *Alles immer smart. Kulturelle Bildung, Digitalisierung, Schule*. Essen: Rat für Kulturelle Bildung e.V.

Strittmatter, Kai. 2018. *Die Neuerfindung der Diktatur: Wie China den digitalen Überwachungsstaat aufbaut und uns damit herausfordert*. München: Piper.

Sudmann, Andreas. 2018a. Zur Einführung. Medien, Infrastrukturen und Technologien des maschinellen Lernens. In *Machine Learning. Medien, Infrastrukturen und Technologien der Künstlichen Intelligenz*, ed. Christoph Engemann and Andreas Sudmann, 9–23. Bielefeld: transcript.

———. 2018b. Szenarien des Postdigitalen. Deep Learning als MedienRevolution. In *Machine learning. Medien, Infrastrukturen und Technologien der Künstlichen Intelligenz*, ed. Christoph Engemann and Andreas Sudmann, 55–73. Bielefeld: transcript.

Taeihagh, Araz. 2017. Crowdsourcing, sharing economies and development. *Journal of Developing Societies* 33 (2): 191–222.

Tang, Audrey. 2019. How to fix democracy. Inside Taiwan's new digital democracy. *The Economist*. https://www.economist.com/openfuture/2019/03/12/inside-taiwans-new-digital-democracy.

———. 2020. The use of the digital fence system is a crucial part of Taiwan's current epidemic prevention measures. *Foundation for Strategic Research* 14 (04): 2020. https://www.frstrategie.org/sites/default/files/documents/publications/autres/2020/Interview%20Audrey%20Tang.pdf.

Tapscott, Don. 2007. *Wikinomics. Die Revolution im Netz*. München: Hanser.

Tegmark, Max. 2017. *Life 3.0. Being human in the age of artificial intelligence*. New York: Alfred A. Knopf.

Telekom. 2016. Telekom Connecting Europe. https://www.youtube.com/watch?v=6No-bDXIdEE.

The Shift Project (TSP): Lean ICT: Towards Digital Sobriety. 2019. https://theshiftproject.org/wp-content/uploads/2019/03/Lean-ICT-Report_The-Shift-Project_2019.pdf.

Thiele, Kathrin. 2015. Ende der Kritik? Kritisches Denken heute. In *Gegen/stand der Kritik*, ed. Andrea Allerkamp, Pablo Valdivia Orozco, and Sophie Witt, 139–162. Zürich/Berlin: Diaphanes.

Thielmann, Tristan. 2018. Early digital images: A praxeology of the display. In *Image–action–space. Situating the screen in visual practice*, ed. Luisa Feiersinger, Kathrin Friedrich, and Moritz Queisner, 41–54. Berlin/Boston: De Gruyter.

Thielmann, Tristan, and Jens Schröter. 2014. Akteur-Medien-Theorie. In *Handbuch Medienwissenschaft*, ed. Jens Schröter, 148–158. Stuttgart/Weimar: Metzler.

Tholen, Georg Christoph. 2002. *Die Zäsur der Medien. Kulturphilosophische Konturen*. Frankfurt a. M: Suhrkamp.

Thomson, William. 1874. Kinetic theory of the dissipation of energy. *Nature* 9: 441–444.

Tiqqun. 2020. *The cybernetic hypothesis*. South Pasadena: Semiotext(e).

Turing, Alan. 1950. Computing machinery and intelligence. *Mind: A Quaterly Review of Psychology and Philosophy* 59 (236): 433–460.

Universal Pictures Home Entertainment. 2019. Good Boys–Trailer. https://www.youtube.com/watch?v=CHD9GoAo59s.

UNESCO. 2019. *I'd blush if I could: Closing gender divides in digital skills through education*. https://unesdoc.unesco.org/ark:/48223/pf0000367416.

van den Boomen, Marianne. 2014. *Transcoding the digital. How metaphors matter in new media*. Amsterdam: Institute of Network Cultures.

Dijck, Van, and José. 2013. *The Culture of connectivity. A critical history of social media*. Oxford: Oxford University Press.

Verhoeff, Nanna. 2012. *Mobile screens. The visual regime of navigation*. Amsterdam: Amsterdam University Press.

Vogl, Joseph. 2021. *Kapital und Ressentiment. Eine kurze Theorie der Gegenwart*. München: C.H. Beck.

von Foerster, Heinz. 1993. *KybernEthik*. Berlin: Merve.

von Gehlen, Dirk. 2020. Durch Corona wird das Internet zur Selbstverständlichkeit. *Süddeutsche Zeitung* 22 (03): 2020. https://sz.de/1.4846552.

von Neumann, John. 1993. Introduction to 'The first draft report on the EDVAC'. *IEEE Annals of the History of Computing* 15 (4): 27–75.

Wan, Evelyn. 2019. Labour, mining, dispossession: On the performance of earth and the necropolitics of digital culture international. *Journal of Performance Arts and Digital Media* 15 (3): 249–263.

Warner Bros. 2019. Neuheiten: Home Video. https://www.warnerbros.de/homevideo/.

Weiland, Michael. 2017. Schnellspur mit Grünstreifen. *Greenpeace* 10 (01): 2017. https://www.greenpeace.de/themen/endlager-umwelt/schnellspur-mit-grunstreifen.

Weiser, Mark. 1994. Building invisible interfaces. *Ubic.Com*. www.ubiq.com/hypertext/weiser/UIST94_4up.ps.

———. 1997. It's everywhere. It's invisible. It's ubicomp. *Training & Development* 51 (5): 34–35.

Weltevrede, Esther, and Fieke Jansen. 2019. Infrastructures of intimate data: Mapping the inbound and outbound data flows of dating apps. *Computational Culture* 7. https://computationalculture.net/infrastructures-of-intimate-data-mapping-the-inbound-and-outbound-data-flows-of-dating-apps/.

Weltkino Filmverleih. 2018. Innenleben–Trailer. https://www.youtube.com/watch?v=82qB4mubdGw.

Wiener, Norbert. 1989. *The human use of human beings: Cybernetics and society*. London: Free Association.

Wilcke, J.C. 1756. *Des Herrn Benjamin Franklins Briefe von der Elektricität*. Leipzig: Gottfried Kiesewetter.

Williams, R. John. 2014. *The Buddha in the machine: Art, technology, and the meeting of east and west*. New Haven: Yale University Press.

Winkler, Hartmut. 2004a. Medium Computer. Zehn populäre Thesen zum Thema und warum sie möglicherweise falsch sind. In *Das Gesicht der Welt. Medien in der digitalen Kultur*, ed. Lorenz Engell and Britta Neitzel, 203–213. München: Fink.

———. 2004. *Diskursökonomie. Versuch über die innere Ökonomie der Medien*. Frankfurt a. M: Suhrkamp.

———. 2015. *Prozessieren. Die dritte, vernachlässigte Medienfunktion*. Paderborn: Fink.

Wirth, Sabine. 2016a. Between interactivity, control, and 'everydayness'– Towards a theory of user interfaces. In *Interface critique*, ed. Florian Hadler and Joachim Haupts, 17–35. Berlin: Kadmos.

———. 2016b. Bericht zum AG-Workshop "Politiken des Interface" (Potsdam). AG Interfaces. https://ag-interfaces.net/2016/07/07/bericht-zum-ag-workshop-politiken-des-interface-potsdam/#more-310.

———. 2019. *Dispositive der Handhabung. Zur Medialität des User Interface*. Dissertation. Philipps-Universität.

Wong, Karen, and Amy Dobson. 2019. We're just data: Exploring China's social credit system in relation to digital platform ratings cultures in westernised democracies. *Global Media and China* 4: 220–232.

Wolfangel, Eva. 2018. Am Ende ist es eine Frage, was die Gesellschaft will. *Der Spiegel* 19 (11): 2018. https://www.spiegel.de/netzwelt/web/projekt-iborderctrl-darf-und-kann-ki-luegner-bei-der-einreise-stoppen-a-1238448.html.

Yoran, Gabriel. 2018. Objects in object-oriented ontology and object-oriented programming. *Interface Critique Journal* 1: 120–133.

Zedler, Johann Heinrich. 1734. *Grosses vollständiges universal-lexicon Aller Wissenschafften und Künste (7. Band)*. Halle/Leipzig: Zedler. https://www.zedler-lexikon.de/.

Zuboff, Shoshana. 2019. *The age of surveillance capitalism. The fight for a human future at the new frontier of power*. New York: Public Affairs.

The manufacturer's authorised representative in the EU is Springer Nature Customer Service Centre GmbH, Europaplatz 3, 69115 Heidelberg, Germany. If you have any concerns regarding our products, please contact ProductSafety@springernature.com

Printed and bound by CPI Group (UK) Ltd, Croydon, CR0 4YY

23/03/2026

02076398-0001